MORE THAN A Butterfly!?

Nathan Cole

More Than A Butterfly!?
By Nathan Cole

www.lulu.com/product/paperback/more-than-a-butterfly/14008733

www.lulu.com/spotlight/necole1979

International Standard Book Number:
978-0-557-85366-3

Lulu Press, Inc.
Printed in United States of America

Special thanks to Robert Carnell, Debbie Waters, and Pammy Martin for their editing help.

Memorial donations can be made to:
Forest Heights Elementary, #1 Learning Place, Gastonia, NC 28052 c/o Susan Cole Fund

Table of Contents

SUSAN COLE
Oct 25 1981 - April 22 2009

Foreword

Susan Cole was not only my younger sister, she was one of my closest friends. Although she was over two years younger than myself, we had a unique bond and special connection similar to that of twins. Since I was three grades ahead of her in school, I kept a close eye on her and made sure I was associated with all her many friends, being the protective brother and all. She was born on a rainy and cool day on October 25, 1981. Like myself, throughout life she enjoyed a wide array of activities. She was a very happy-go-lucky girl who did not let much bother her, even though she seemed to have a hassle with everything. Her unique, child-like personality was very appropriate and beneficial in her job as a More at Four teacher. She loved her students as if they were her own children, and she brightened everyone's day. Her Jack Russell, Rufus, was also very special to her and he loved her like everyone else who came in contact with Susan. Whether she was making some outlandish comment, a quirky upside down smile, or simply being there as a friend; everyone loved being around Susan. Before Susan became a teacher at Forest Heights Elementary in Gastonia, North Carolina, she graduated from Chase High in 2000 and UNC-Greensboro in 2004. She also became a Christian at a young age while attending Floyd's Creek Baptist Church. All who had the opportunity of knowing Susan were

extremely blessed and fortunate. She had a persona about her that could brighten the cloudiest of days. She was always the one I wanted to call if I needed an encouraging word or just to hear a friendly voice.

It is amazing at how many lives she was able to touch, affect, and change in such a short time frame. There is not a day that goes by that she is not missed, thought about, and remembered! We will always love her. There is no doubt Susan was a very special girl who was taken way too young.

Introduction

April 18th, 2009 started out like any other ordinary day, but it would turn out to be anything but ordinary. It was a beautiful spring morning and I woke up around 8:00 like I did every morning to get ready for work. This was supposed to be a short day at work since I was heading to Alabama for our company meeting early the next morning. I would leave work early this day, but unfortunately not for the reason I had initially planned. Around 12:40, I received a call that I would never forget. This is an account of some of my thoughts, experiences, and reflections I dealt with during the next eighteen months.

MORE THAN A BUTTERFLY!?

Chapter 1. It's Just A Butterfly!

"Come on, we're going to be late for church. What are you doing? What's taking you so long? You know I hate to be late. Where are you, Susan?"

"I'm on the porch, Nathan. Look at that butterfly. It's so pretty. Solid black, with just a little purple on it's wings."

"What are you talking about? I ain't got time to look at that. We're going to be late, Susan. You know it's Easter Sunday and the church will be packed. We can't be late today or we won't have a seat. I ain't sitting in the balcony."

"Alright, I'm coming. Just chill out why don't you?"

"Whatever, let's just go."

"What took you so long?" Mom asked.

"Nothing, I was just looking at a butterfly on the porch."

"Well I hope a butterfly doesn't make us late for church. You know how many people flock out for church on Easter Sunday."

"We ain't going to be late…we have

plenty of time to get there."

"Look Mom, the parking lot is not even full yet."

"Hey Ann, it's good to see you today. How's Marcus doing? I hear he's about to have a baby."

"Yea, they are really excited. I am too…can't wait to have another grandchild. It's good to see you, Susan. Are you still working with kids?"

"Yea…still doing More at Four in Gastonia."

"That's great! Y'all were running a little behind today."

"Yea…Susan had to look at a butterfly."

"It wasn't just a butterfly!"

They had so many announcements today. My back was killing me having to stand up during all of them. You would think they could have at least let us sit down. I'm surprised how many they had on Easter Sunday. Well, at least we get to go over to Granny's house for lunch today. "Did you bring a change of clothes, Susan?"

"Of course…I ain't wearing my dress all day."

"Well, I brought one too, even though I love being all dressed up. Don't want to be the only one at Granny's dressed up. Is everyone going to be there today?"

"As far as I know they will."

"That's good. Ever since I got engaged last month, Wesley has been asking me random questions about rings. He will probably talk to me about them again today. I think he's about ready to pop the question or he's just real weird about diamonds."

"Looks like we're the first ones here again."

"Yea…everyone else probably went home to change first. Nathan, can you help me with the food? Just set it on the table and I'll arrange it later. Everyone else will be here shortly."

"Emily and Shane just pulled up. Hello Embo, long time no see."

"Hello Susie Q, how's it going?"

"Pretty good, I took an IQ test this week and it said I was a genius."

"Is that a fact?"

"Yea…it's been obvious for a while, but that just proved it."

"Well, you must be getting a little smarter,… you did go see the Tarheels win the National Championship."

"I know it Shane, I've been all over the world this week."

"Well, the only reason I pull for them is it helps with sales. You remember what happened after they won it in '93. I can't believe it's April again. It's hard to believe it has been sixteen years."

Chapter 2. UNC Vs. Michigan

"Listen up everyone!!! Students, students, be quiet. I know you're all excited because it's March Madness time again, but you must keep your voices down. This year I've decided to let everyone fill out a bracket, and the winner gets an extra 100 for the semester. I need everyone's bracket by Thursday or you will be disqualified from the contest."

"Hey Chad! Who you got winning it all this year?"

"You know I'm picking the Tarheels."

"Are you crazy? Have you even seen Duke play this year? I mean heck, Michigan has the Fab Five. There are so many teams that can win it this year. Not only does Duke and Michigan look tough, but Kentucky or Kansas can easily beat the Tarheels too. Well, you can pick them if you want, but I need that extra 100 so I'm going to pick the best team."

"And who exactly is that?"

"Duh, Duke of course. How can you go wrong with Grant Hill, Christian Laettner, and Bobby Hurly?"

"Well, you know Duke can't win it three years in a row."

****

"So Chad, how'd you do after the first round of play?"

"Well, the Tarheels are still in it. Other

than that I only picked twenty-three total games right."

"That ain't too bad. I have twenty-six teams still in it. Missed a couple of upsets though. I heard Natalie picked thirty-one out of thirty-two games. That's crazy. I sure as heck ain't getting beat by a girl."

"Yea, I know whatcha mean."

"So you got any big plans this weekend?"

"Nah, not really. Me and my brother, Shane, may shoot a little ball. Might just lay around watching ballgames all weekend."

"Must be nice. Don't forget about that big math test Mrs. Petty is giving us Monday."

"I ain't really worried about it. When are we ever going to need algebra again?"

"For real, but I need an A on this one since it counts half our grade."

"Oh well, good luck with that, and go watch Duke get beat this weekend."

"Whatever, they are playing California. That'll be a blow out."

****

"So what happened to your Blue Devils?"

"Don't get me started about that game. I ain't never seen someone go off like Jason Kidd did. Who would have thought Duke would have gotten beat by a freshman. Of course, we did win the past two years, and y'all ain't won since '82 when y'all had Jordan."

"Wait and see, this is Carolina's year "

"So how many teams you got left in your bracket, Chad?"

"I ain't got but seven, but the Tarheels are still there."

"Well I got Carolina still too, but I have Arkansas beating them in the next game. Natalie has still got thirteen teams left. She don't even know anything about basketball."

"I know it. You shooting ball this afternoon?"

"Nah, I got senior league tryouts at Crowe Park."

"Well, have fun, and hit a homer."

****

"Down to the Final Four, Chad. You got any teams left?"

"I told you I picked Carolina to win it all. I actually picked all four of the teams left."

"That's crazy. I just have Michigan left. Of course, I had them getting beat by Duke so I ain't going to win anyways."

"Yea, I think it's down to me and Natalie. She's only got two teams left though, Carolina and Kansas. She's picked fifty-one games right so far and I've picked fifty. So if Carolina beats Kansas and Michigan beats Kentucky we will be tied going into the final game."

"Since I can't win, I hope you beat her."

"Yea, me too. We would never live it down if we get beat by a girl."

"Well Chad, you got your wish, down to Carolina and Michigan for the National Championship."

"I know it, man. Should be a good game, but I think Carolina will win. If they do, then I'll beat Natalie since she picked Duke to beat Carolina."

"Well, I'm sure I'll watch it, but I'll be tired after my first baseball practice of the year. Although I didn't get on Eric's team, I'll probably give him a call after practice. After all, he's a big Tarheel fan as well."

"I ain't heard from Eric in a while, how's he doing?"

"He's good…hard to believe it's been three years since he's been at our school."

****

"I can't believe how that game ended last night. First of all, Weber walked way before calling a timeout he didn't have. They wouldn't have even been there without him, but how can you make such a huge mistake in such a big game? I'll give Carolina credit, they played well, but I still think Michigan was the better team."

"Yea, yea, that's what all Duke fans say. I bet Eric loved it."

"Yea, he called as soon as it was over to rub it in my face. I jokingly told him to call after they won two in a row. He optimistically said, 'Just wait till next year.' I'm spending the night with him Friday, so I'm sure he's going to give me a hard time."

Chapter 3. Different Plans For The Weekend

Tarheel fans sure love to rub it in your face when they win. They didn't have much to say the past two years. Oh well, there's always next year for Duke. I'm just glad baseball season is back in full force. This is my second year at Crowe Park. I don't like it as good as Cliffside since I don't know anyone. The only reason I decided to play there was because Eric began playing there once he moved, and I'm not even on his team. I sure hope they call off practice today; it's cold and rainy, plus I have lots of homework. I haven't heard any word yet, so I guess it's still on as scheduled. I wonder why everyone's just standing around talking. Maybe they decided to cancel practice since it's a little drizzly.

"Dad, what are those people talking about, WHO DIED, WHO?"

"No one from our team, a kid from Fast Foods."

"That's the team Eric plays on. Tell me it's not...OH NO! NOT ERIC!"

The ride home was a blur, but yet so clear. Stephanie had just gotten her license a few months back, so Dad drove her car, a teal 1990 Geo Storm. Greg and Tim Chapman's parents dropped them off so when practice was cancelled, they wanted us to give them a ride home. Of course we did. I sat in the back with

Tim, didn't speak, didn't cry. I was completely emotionless. They got out and thanked us for the ride. Was I even there? I don't remember. Before going home we stopped by Eric's house. I saw his sister, Leslie. She had a drink in her hand; I hugged her and can still hear the ice shake in her cup. I don't remember seeing his parents. There were so many people at his house. I felt like if they saw me they would think of him…we were so alike. As we were leaving his house, I saw a butterfly float through the air. I thought to myself, how can anything look so peaceful when I am hurting so bad? Why do our lives have to be so difficult and a simple butterfly can look so happy?

We arrived home shortly after visiting his family. Momma, Stephanie, and Susan were eating supper - chicken pot pies. I haven't had a pot pie since. Mom wondered if practice was cancelled because of the weather. I could barely speak. I was able to mutter, "Eric's dead."

"What, what?"

Through tear-filled words I mumbled, "He was shot and killed." All I remember after that was Susan staring at me and Stephanie crying. I kept thinking…is this real, is this a dream? However, it was real; it wasn't a dream! How could life go on after this moment in time? I went to bed that night but wasn't tired. I was exhausted but couldn't sleep. How could someone be exhausted, yet not be tired? How could this be, we were only thirteen? No one dies this young! I was going to spend the night

with him on Friday. I'd talked to him less than twenty-four hours before. I lay in bed for hours. I must have eventually cried myself to sleep, because in what seemed like fifteen minutes my mom was waking me up for school. How could I possibly go to school this day? What would people say to me? What would I say to them? A thirteen year old couldn't answer these questions. A thirteen year old shouldn't have to answer these questions.

The next day at school everyone was looking at me. What were they wanting to hear? What did they want me to say? Were they surprised to see me the day after my best friend was killed? Natalie came up to me and hugged me. She handed me a letter and said, "I want you to read this to the school." How could I do that when I could not speak? I opened my mouth and there was a lump in my throat. What if I cry? I couldn't show emotion. But I had to…I had to do this for Eric. Chad and I went to raise the flag that morning like we had so many times in the past. However, today was different...today, my best friend was dead!

I earnestly told Chad we needed to raise the flag only half-way in honor of my friend. He surprisingly responded, "We can't without Mr. Beam's permission."

I wouldn't raise the flag the rest of the year.

I took the folded note out of my pocket and read over it. Tears welled up in my eyes. I tried to gather myself but how…my best friend

was dead. I went into the office, got over the intercom, and tearfully began to read the words written by my best friend's family.

> "On July 26, 1979, God gave to our family a very special gift. We called his name Eric Matthew Poteat and what a special joy He had sent to our lives. For nearly fourteen years we were able to share many precious and happy times, times that we will always treasure. On April 6, 1993, God chose to call our special gift back home to be with Him. Now our hearts are filled with sorrow because of the desire to see his face, to hear his voice, to see his smile, and to hold him in our arms, but we don't sorrow as those who have no hope, for we know that we will see him again in Heaven. Words cannot express to each of you how much the love and kindness shown to our family during this time of our lives has meant. Thank you for every prayer, flower, card, telephone call, gifts to the van fund, and every nice word about our precious son. We love you Eric. Thank you, the family of Eric Poteat."

I went back to my social studies class with Mr. Womack and asked if he had heard about Eric dying. He regretfully informed me he had heard the bad news. That evening I went home, but again couldn't eat or sleep. I lay in

bed crying for hours. I had to cry while lying in bed…I couldn't cry when people were watching me, waiting for me to break down. How many nights would this go on? How long would I be hurting from the loss of my best friend?

The next night was the receiving of friends at Harrelson Funeral Home. There were so many people in line. Mrs. Hoyle and Mrs. Hall, our kindergarten teachers, were just ahead of me in line. I could still remember playing with him in kindergarten like it was yesterday. Such a peaceful, care-free time of life. That's the way it should be as kids; that's the way it still should be. Life doesn't seem so peaceful anymore. I guess we weren't invincible like we thought…like all kids think. After over three hours in line, I finally got to the coffin. He was wearing a Florida Marlins jersey; this was their first year in the league. He would never get to see them play! He would never get to grow up! Life's not fair! Why, why did this have to happen to my best friend?

It was Friday now...but not just any Friday, this was Good Friday. Hard to see anything good about this day. I left school early on yet another rainy day. Guess even the angels in Heaven were crying today. Natalie rode with us to the funeral. We rode in our white mini van. Natalie and I were in the back seat. She had on a black dress, only appropriate for one going to a funeral. As she was getting out of the van, one of the buttons to her dress popped off. I often wonder what ever happened to that button. I

haven't been back to his grave. Hard to find any comfort in seeing where my best friend was buried.

"I hope I can sleep tonight." It had been three days since my best friend was tragically killed. I had not been able to eat or sleep. I was so exhausted, but yet still couldn't fall asleep. I lay in bed for a while. I began to pray. I closed my eyes still thinking about Eric. I opened my eyes to see my bedspread covered with a bright neon green glow. I must have been dreaming. This couldn't be real. Was this real? What is real? I tried to touch the glow but couldn't before falling asleep. I woke up some eight hours later. Had I slept through the night? Was the glow on my bed real? I couldn't tell anybody. They would think I was crazy. Maybe I was crazy. However, wasn't it crazy…Eric, my best friend, was killed at thirteen. Wasn't it crazy I'll never play with him or see him again.

Chapter 4. What's Next?

Well…it had been almost a week since Eric died, and it was time for spring break. We've had our family vacation planned for a while, so we decided to keep our reservations. How could I possibly enjoy a vacation when I was still mourning the death of my best friend? He wasn't just a friend…he was like a brother. I don't remember much about this vacation, other than it was cold. There was lots of silence on the way down to our hotel. Maybe people were talking, and I just couldn't hear past my thoughts. Obviously, I only had one thing on my mind, and that one thing would stay on mind for years.

Spring break had come, and spring break had gone. The flowers were blooming, the air was warming, and the butterflies were fluttering beautifully through the cool sky. Time to face the reality of school once again. Less than two months now until summer break…my last summer break before high school. Things would be different. People say you'll make new friends. Was that supposed to console me? Was that supposed to make me feel better? I passed my old friends in the hall. Were they still my friends? Did they see me differently now? I mean, I still saw them as friends. However, it was not the same; it never will be. My best friend was gone; however, not just to a different school this time, but gone for good, gone forever. I was only thirteen years old. How could I live

the rest of my life without my best friend? Whom was I supposed to play with, hang out with, or talk to about girls?

Finally, the last week of school. The last time I would be a student at Tri-Community. Lots had happened these past five years. I had met lots of great friends; however, I had lost a few as well. I passed Gary in the hall once again, the third of the Three Stooges. Hard to believe all we had left were our memories. We would never be the Three Stooges again. All that practice and hard work creating a skit. Haha, it sure was fun though. We had a time together! Did I remind him of Eric like he did me? Would we continue to be friends, or was it just going to be too hard staying close to anyone who was associated with me and Eric?

It was time for our annual award ceremony again. Last full day of school. Finally!!! I wondered if I would win any awards this year. I mean, did I even do any school work the past two months? It was such a blur. I guess I completed all my assignments.

"Good afternoon faculty, students, family, and friends. As you know, today is the last day of school and time for our annual awards ceremony. I'm pleased to announce we had a record number of award winners this year. Mrs. Elliott and Mr. Womack are going to assist me with the awards. Please hold your applause until all names have been called. We will begin with the eighth grade class. We had five perfect attendance students from the eighth grade this

year: Matt Bridges, Natalie Byers, Nathan Cole, Christy Lee, and Chad Robbins. 2nd place in Science - Natalie Byers, 1st place - Nathan Cole. 2nd place in English - Nathan Cole, 1st place - Matt Bridges. 2nd place in Math - Natalie Byers, 1st place - Nathan Cole. 2nd place in Social Studies - Matt Bridges, 1st place - Nathan Cole. 2nd place in P.E. - Chad Robbins, 1st place - Jayvon McKinney."

Wow! I'm surprised I won so many awards this year. Now it was time for high school. It was going to be a lot different at Chase then it was at Tri-Community. At least my sister, Stephanie, would be there my first couple of years. Maybe that would help me adjust. I hope so, because "I feel like I ain't got a friend in the world."

Chapter 5: Carolina Wins Again

Michigan State versus North Carolina. This seemed eerily similar to the championship game in '93 when UNC beat Michigan. I hated to see the Tarheels win again, but it sure would help sales. Seemed like it had been forever since I had actually hit a sales goal two months in a row. Just think, three years ago I was one of the top sales gainers for the entire company, and now I was pulling for Carolina just to make a bonus.

"Wow Kyra, that game wasn't even close last night. Guess we better be ready for an extremely busy next few days. We'll go ahead and start making a list of names and numbers for the customers wanting the championship shirts."

"What time do you think the shirts will be in?"

"Melony said she'd be here by lunch time. I'd tell people around 3 or 4 just in case though."

"That's the 100th person who's called wanting those shirts, and it's not even lunch time yet!"

"I know it, they better get here soon or we're going to have a lot of angry customers. There's over twenty people waiting around for them, and I told them it may be a couple hours."

"They don't care as long as they get one! I'm not even sure how many we are getting. Melony just pulled up. Finally, this won't take long to sell. Start asking people for sizes, and I'll

separate them out."

"I can't believe we sold all 120 shirts in less than an hour. That is absolutely insane."

"We still have nearly fifty people on our waiting list. What are we supposed to do?"

"Just tell them I'm going to make another trip to Shelby tonight, and we'll have them here around 7. Then we'll have another shipment arrive around lunch time tomorrow and the following day."

"Wow…this was a crazy busy week."

"Yep! We made nearly $5,000 just on Tarheel merchandise, not to mention how much we did from baseball sales. We needed a week like that. Of course, we were up last month due mainly in part to Carolina winning so much. It's always nice when you start the month off as strong as we have. Hopefully, we can ride the Tarheels success for the rest of this month. Well, y'all are going to have to do it without me for about a week."

"Oh yea, you're going to Alabama on Saturday."

"Yea, I can't wait. Even though it's work, it's kind of relaxing."

"What time are y'all leaving?"

"I don't think we are going to leave until early Sunday morning, but we're trying to convince her to let us leave Saturday night. I don't want to have to wake up at the crack of dawn. Y'all hold down the fort for me."

Chapter 6. Nelson's Birthday

"Seems like Tarheel sales are finally slowing down. Probably a good thing, since we don't have much left anyways. I'm about ready for a few days in Alabama. Try to recoup from these past couple of crazy months and get reenergized for the upcoming back to school rush."

"Were you able to convince Melony into leaving tomorrow?"

"Nah…I think we've decided to meet in Greenville at 6 a.m. on Sunday. It won't be any fun getting up at that time of day. I'll have to leave my house by at least 4:45 in the morning. That's way too early to be getting up! I didn't even realize that time came more than once a day. Oh well!"

"So have you packed yet, or are you waiting till the last minute like most guys?"

"Haven't started yet. I'm going to leave work around lunch time tomorrow and throw some things together. Shouldn't take me but a half an hour to get packed."

"You get off at 5:30 tonight, right?"

"Yea…going out to eat for my brother-in-law's birthday."

"That'll be fun. Where are y'all going?"

"This little Japanese place in Shelby called Sushi Dojo. I haven't ever been there before. Hopefully, it'll be good. It should be…I love Japanese and he loves sushi."

"Hey Mom, we ended up getting busy right before I got off tonight. Seems like every time I have somewhere to be we get slammed. Oh well, let me change clothes and brush my teeth, then I'll be ready. We'll still have plenty of time to get there. It only takes around twenty-five minutes."

"Yea, hurry up though."

****

"Looks like Susan has beat us here, there's her jeep. Yea, I see her waving us into a parking space."

"Hello Holmes! How goes it?"

"Pretty good Gay Johnny, what have you been up to?"

"Not much, just been around the world."

"That's what I hear; can't believe you're actually starting to pull for Carolina."

"Where's Sister Ethel and N. Long?"

"They should be here anytime, probably just running a couple minutes behind. I'm going to go ahead and put our name on the list to get us a table."

"Hello. Welcome to Sushi Dojo; I'm Ashley, I'll be serving you guys tonight. Can I start by getting everyone's drink orders?"

"Water, water, water, water, water, water with lemon, please."

"Alright, I have six waters, 1 with lemon. Would anyone else care for a lemon?"

"I would, please."

"I'll be right back with your drinks, and then I'll get your orders."

A few minutes later…"Has everyone decided what they would like tonight?"

"I think so."

"Alright, we will start with you and work our way around."

"Come back to me last. Mine's different from everyone else's." Nelson explained.

"Teriyaki chicken."

"I'm going to have the same."

"Me too."

"Hibachi chicken. Can I get extra mushrooms, please?"

"I'll take Hibachi chicken as well. Thanks."

"Have you decided what you would like?" "Yes, I'm going to have the Sushi Sampler."

"That comes with tuna, salmon, crab, and shrimp. Is that fine?"

"That's good, and can I add an order of Mackerel?"

"Alright, is there anything else I can get you guys tonight?"

"I think that's going to do it, thanks."

"I'll put this order in and get it out as quickly as possible. I'll bring you some more water too."

"Thank you!"

"I don't understand why, on Facebook, you can 'like' someone's status, but you can't

'dislike' it."

"I'm pretty sure you can 'dislike' or 'like' someone's status, Susan."

"I tried to 'dislike' someone's the other day but couldn't."

"I'm not positive about that…I'll have to check into it. Are you going to spend the night with us since you're going to the wedding tomorrow?"

"No, Jesse is coming with me, so I'm going to pick him up in the morning and come down then. I may stop by before the wedding since it ain't until 4."

"You should just stay and have him come down tomorrow since we don't get to see you much."

"Well, I'll be home again next weekend for Granny's birthday."

We left the restaurant shortly before 8 and gathered outside for a few moments. It was just before dark, and we were making small conversation. I then noticed several butterflies fluttering through the air. Susan made a comment about how amazing it was such a beautiful creature used to be little more than a caterpillar. She was right…they were very beautiful and peaceful.

I arrived home and checked my Facebook once again. I then realized for some reason you could only 'like' someone's status. Seemed kind of strange you couldn't 'dislike' someone's status as well. However, I wanted to share my discovery with my sister so I texted her.

"Susan, I was wrong u can unlike ur like but can't dislike - proverbs 3:5-6."

"What?"

"On Facebook."

"OK."

Chapter 7. Selling A Ball Goal

"I'm surprised it's been so slow today, Samantha."

"I know, I guess the Tarheel mania has finally wore off."

"Yea…I'm kind of glad though. I'm needing to leave around lunch time anyways to get ready for my trip tomorrow. Got to be in Greenville at 6 a.m."

"Wow…that's early!"

"Once Candace gets here I'll send you on break, and then I'm going to head out."

I answered the phone, "It's a great day! This is Nathan. How may I help you?"

"I am interested in buying a basketball goal."

"Alright, are you looking for an inground or portable?"

"What are the advantages?"

"Well, a portable would be good if you were planning on moving or if you wanted to transport the goal easily. As far as an inground, it's usually a little cheaper since you don't need the base, and there is less chance of it tipping over in a bad storm."

"I'm not planning on moving anytime soon, so I guess the inground would be best for me."

"Ok, let me check to see which ones we have in stock, and I'll be right back. Ma'am, I have two different styles in stock. Both are made

by Lifetime and have a five-year warranty. I have one on sale for $149.99 with a 44" backboard and is made out of fiberglass. The other is $349.99 with a 48" backboard made out of acrylic."

"What are the advantages of getting one that much more expensive?"

"Well, acrylic is the strongest type backboard we carry and will be much less likely to crack than fiberglass. The official size of backboards are 48" as well. This will allow your kids the true feel for the correct size backboard they will be playing on during games. Both of these goals are also 20% off right now."

"Thanks for your help…I'll be by to check them out shortly."

"Thank you, and see you later." I hung up the phone as Candace arrived to work.

"Hey Candace, how are you?"

"I'm tired, I stayed up way too late last night."

"Well, at least it's been fairly slow today. Samantha, you can go on break since Candace is here."

"Alright, I'll be in the back eating my lunch if you get busy."

"Thanks, but I'm pretty sure we can handle it today. Haha."

Once again I answered the phone, "It's a great day! This is Nathan. How may I help you?"

"Hey, what time are you planning on coming home today?"

"I'll probably leave by 1. Samantha just went on break, and I'm waiting on this lady to come pick up a basketball goal."

"Well, Susan has been in a wreck, and they are taking her to the hospital."

"Alright, I'm on my way up there right now. I'll talk to you later, Mom."

As I hung up the phone, I uttered, "My sister has just been in a wreck, Candace. I got to go!"

"Are you going to be ok? Do you need me to drive you? You don't need to drive if you're upset!"

"I'll be fine Candace, thanks. I'm going to go tell Samantha and then head out."

I went to the backroom and frantically told Samantha, "I got to go…my sister has been in a wreck. There ain't no one in the store right now, so finish eating. I just wanted to let you know before I left."

"Do you need anything? Are you going to be alright?"

"I'm sure it'll be fine; I just need to go. By the way, a lady is supposed to come look at an inground ball goal in a little while."

"Ok, call us when you can, and let us know how she is."

"Thanks, I'll see you later."

"Hey Melony, this is Nathan. I'm on my way to the hospital. My sister has been in a wreck. I don't have any details yet, but I need to check on her and wanted to let you know I'm

leaving the store. I should still be able to go to Alabama tomorrow, but I'll let you know when I have more details."

"Alright, I hope everything is fine."

"Thank you."

Before I arrived at the hospital I prayed to God begging everything would be alright. I didn't audibly get a response back, but I did see a butterfly while walking into the hospital. I thought to myself…Jesus created every beautiful creature in this world and has a perfect plan for everyone.

Chapter 8. Waiting For News

After I got off the phone with Melony, different scenarios kept popping through my head. I didn't know why, but all I kept thinking was her jeep turned over on the side and she had broken her arm. I didn't know if she had gotten her seatbelt fixed or not. I bet Rufus distracted her and caused her to lose control of her jeep. Was God punishing me for something I had done? Was He punishing her? I knew I had prayed for Susan and Jesse not to get married, but never in a million years would I have wanted anything bad to happen to them.

"Hey, I'm here to see Susan Cole. She was in a wreck."

"Let's see. I don't have a Susan Cole here."

"She was with her boyfriend, Jesse. It was a car wreck."

"No one by those names are here yet. When did it happen?"

"Just a few minutes ago."

"You've probably just beaten the ambulance here. They should arrive soon."

"Have you heard how they are doing?"

"I haven't. Of course, that's not unusual. We usually just hear when they are admitted. Just have a seat, and as soon as I hear something I'll let you know."

"Thanks."

I anxiously awaited any news on how she

was doing. Finally! An ambulance pulled up. That had to be her!

"Has Susan been admitted yet; I just saw an ambulance pull up?"

"Nope, not yet. Let me call someone and see if I can find out something."

"Thank you."

How could she possibly not be at the hospital yet; it had been nearly half an hour? I sat back down. There was a couple sitting next to me with a radio. I wasn't paying much attention, lost in my own thoughts. I casually overheard, "two injured in motorcycle wreck, one with major head trauma." Motorcycle! That couldn't be them…could it? She was in her jeep with Rufus. Why would she be on a motorcycle? She didn't ride bikes, much less motorcycles. She didn't even like them. She was always afraid when Teddy used to ride his up and down the street. Stop thinking like that! That was a different wreck…that couldn't have been her.

"They don't know where she is, Momma."

"What do you mean?"

"She ain't here."

"They've got to be here by now. It's been almost an hour."

"I know, I've been here for over forty-five minutes and haven't gotten any word yet. You'd think they would know where she is by now."

"I know it."

Shortly after, my phone rang. "Hello."

"Hey Nathan, what's going on? I saw your car in the parking lot and just passed your parents."

"Susan was in a wreck, Melvin. I've been up here for about forty-five minutes and haven't gotten any word yet. She's not here, and they don't know where she is, or how she's doing. I'll let you know something as soon as I hear anything. Thanks for calling."

"If you need anything just let me know."

"I definitely will."

****

"Mr. and Mrs. Cole, I'm Chris St. Claire; I was the first responder at the scene."

"Is she alright? Can we see her? Where is she?"

"Well, she and Jesse were in a motorcycle wreck."

"A motorcycle! She wasn't in her jeep?"

"No, Jesse is here but we had to airlift Susan to Missions Memorial in Asheville."

"Oh No! Is she alright?"

"She was alert and speaking at the scene. They were talking about the wedding."

"Was she wearing a helmet?"

"That's inconclusive. She didn't have it on when I arrived at the scene, but there were helmets on the ground."

"Was she crying?"

"No, she didn't seem to be in much pain. I was able to have a conversation with her, like I am with you right now. When the ambulance

arrived she did become a little combative and was complaining of knee pain."

"Why did you have to airlift her to Asheville then?"

"Her stomach was a little bloated and her blood pressure was fluctuating. That's common in a traumatic event, and I don't think there is anything to worry about."

All I could think about was what I heard over that radio. That had to be the wreck Susan was in. If they airlifted Susan…the one with head trauma had to be her. If it wasn't then they would have airlifted Jesse.

"Let's go back to see Jesse before we pick up Stephanie to go to Asheville." Dad said.

"Alright, but let's hurry; I want to get up there as soon as we can."

"Hey Jesse, how you feeling?"

"I have a headache, and my arm is hurting real bad. I'm sorry!!! I didn't mean to hurt her."

"Everything is going to be fine. Did you have your helmets on?"

"Yes!"

"What happened?"

"I don't really know; I just lost control of the bike."

The nurse came in…"I'm going to take your blood pressure real quick, Jesse."

"Ok, can I have some water?"

"We're going to go see Susan, you take care of yourself." Dad politely said.

"OK, I'm so sorry!"

Jesse was covered in blood, and I kept

thinking if he looked this bad…how bad must Susan look. After all, she was the one they decided to airlift to Asheville. It was going to be a long drive to Asheville, and time seemed to be creeping.

"Nathan, go ahead and call Shane to get a prayer chain started."

A prayer chain? Was it going to be that bad? I hope not…I pray not!

"Shane, this is Nathan whatcha up to?"

"Not much."

"Susan's been in a wreck. They airlifted her to Asheville. We're on our way up there now."

"Have you heard how she is?"

"I haven't gotten any word yet. The first responder said her stomach was swelling, her blood pressure was fluctuating, and she was being combative. I'll let you know when we hear more. Could you go ahead and start a prayer chain for us?"

"Of course, let me know if there is anything else I can do."

"Thanks Shane. I'll talk to you soon."

Chapter 9. 5th Floor

"Stephanie, Susan's been in a wreck, and they airlifted her to Asheville. We thought she was at Rutherfordton and didn't find out otherwise for over an hour. We're leaving the hospital now, and we will pick you up in a few minutes to make the trip up to Asheville."

"Alright, I'll see you in a little while."

"Hey Stephanie, you ready to go?"

"Yea…I've been ready to see Susan."

"Can I get something to drink and a pack of crackers first? I just got off the golf course and haven't eaten lunch."

"Hurry up Dad…I'm ready to see how Susan's doing!"

It felt like it took forever to get up to Asheville. I knew it only took about forty minutes from Rutherfordton, but that was a very long forty minutes. I mean, you would think Dad could at least have gone the speed limit. Did he not want to see her? Was he expecting the worse? Finally…we arrived! What will we find?

I rushed in ahead of everyone else. I didn't know where to go, but I was determined to find her. The not knowing was unbearable. Finally, I saw the receptionist and frantically said, "I'm here to see Susan Cole…I'm her brother." Mom, Dad, and Stephanie had caught up to me by now. The receptionist directed us to the 5th floor, the neuro-trauma unit.

Neuro-trauma, that's the brain! She looked at us kind of weird, like we should have known that. How could we…we were told she was having stomach bloating? What does that have to do with the brain? I found the elevator and pressed five till it lit up. It was almost 4 p.m. by now. Nearly three hours had passed since the accident at 12:03 p.m. Was she going to be all right? Was it too late?

Finally I got up to the dreaded 5th floor. Surely, we were getting close to finding her now. We walked up and down the empty hall. I couldn't find anyone. It was Saturday, but surely someone was working. Surely someone knew where Susan was…how Susan was. After what seemed like forever, we came to a waiting room full of people. There was a desk with a phone but no nurse. I've got to find Susan. Every second felt like an hour, every hour like a day. Time seemed to have stopped. I picked up the phone, but who was I supposed to call? How was I supposed to know how to find my sister? By this time I was hysterical. I cried out, "Does anyone know where my sister is?" People were looking at us but not speaking. A young lady finally came up to me and asked, "What's going on?" I frantically told her my sister had been in a motorcycle wreck, and I was informed she was in the neuro-trauma unit. She teared up; her father had been in a motorcycle wreck earlier in the week and she'd be able to direct us where to go.

"Follow me, I'll help you find your sister!"

Chapter 10. Stable But Critical

It was 4:30 p.m. now. We still hadn't seen Susan. The doctor took us into a room and explained to us about Susan's injuries.

"Mr. and Mrs. Cole, I'm Dr. Thompson; I've been examining your daughter. She's a very sick little girl. Currently, she is stable but critical." Stable but critical, what's that even mean?

"The next seventy-two hours will be vital. We've gotten the results back from her initial CAT scan, and it came back negative, which is a good sign. However, she does have a class 3 left kidney injury, a class 3 liver injury, and a class 4 spleen injury. To further explain what this means, all injuries are categorized into classes. There are five classes, class 5 being the most serious. Anything over a class 3 can be life-threatening. Susan has three separate life-threatening injuries to her internal organs. Here are some pictures of Susan's internal organs and I'm sure you can see how severe these injuries are."

I'm no expert, but even I could tell how much damage had been done. Her organs looked like someone had thrown a tomato against the wall. I hopefully asked, "Can we see her?"

"Yes, I'll let the nurses know you are here and let you come on back."

While I was waiting to go see my sister, all I kept thinking about was I would gladly give

her a kidney. I would gladly do anything if it would help save my sister. We were so alike; surely there was something I could do to help her. I kept remembering Chris saying she wasn't in much pain. How could that possibly be with all her injuries? When we were finally able to see her, she had been sedated and placed in a self-induced coma. I couldn't help but think…if only we had gotten here sooner would we be able to speak to her? Would she be able to tell us what happened?

Finally, 4:50 p.m. and we were able to see my sister. We had to sanitize our hands when we walked into the neuro-trauma unit. I didn't mind; I was just glad to finally see Susan. Jennifer was Susan's first nurse when we arrived. Even after all of Dr. Thompson's assessments, I was still very optimistic. Jennifer explained to us they had put her in a comatose state so she would be unable to pull any tubes out and further hurt herself. Hard to imagine her being able to hurt herself further. We informed the nurse that Susan wore contacts so Jennifer took them out and gave Momma her engagement ring. She then explained that on the initial tests Susan seemed to be moving both legs and her right arm well but was struggling moving her left arm. I let her know she was in a skiing accident a while back and had been having trouble with her left elbow popping out of joint. Jennifer further explained since the left hemisphere of the brain controls the right side of the body, most right handed head trauma victims survive with minimal problems.

Simultaneously, we all yelled, “She’s left handed!” I thought at that time, “Head trauma? Didn’t her CAT scan come back good?”

Jennifer told us she was about to reassess Susan’s vital signs and asked if we would like to stay in. Of course, it took us so long to find her I didn’t want to leave now. “I’m going to take her out of the induced coma and reexamine her.” It only took a few minutes for her to come out of the comatose state. Susan opened her eyes for about five seconds, looked around, and began moaning in what seemed to be agonizing pain. Jennifer then got a flashlight and began shining it in Susan’s eyes. There was no response, and I saw tears gather in Jennifer’s eyes. It wasn’t until then I knew how bad this situation was. At this time, it was recommended we wait outside.

How could she be so bad? She had minimal cuts, scrapes, or bruises. I guess what they say is true: “What’s on the inside is what counts!”

The nurse gave us two brochures explaining the rules and hours of the neuro-trauma unit. Visiting hours: fifteen minutes each, four times a day, two people at a time.

Wow…how could we only spend an hour a day visiting my sister? What would I say to her? Could she hear me? Could she feel me squeeze her hand? What was she thinking? Was she still there? Was she in pain? So many questions, so few answers!

Chapter 11. Spreading The News

So many people I had to call. So many things I had to say. What should I say? Who should I call? "Shane, hey this is Nathan, just wanted to give you an update on Susan. Her initial CAT scan came back negative, which is good. However, her organs are very messed up. The doctor explained she has three life-threatening injuries to her internal organs, and the next seventy-two hours would be critical. If you could spread the news for me and tell everyone to pray, I would appreciate it."

"Ok, me and Emily will head up for a while tonight."

"Thanks, I'll cya soon."

"Hey Melony, I was wanting to let you know my sister ain't doing well at all. They have her in a self-induced coma right now. It's not looking good. She's at Mission Memorial in Asheville. I doubt I'll be able to go to Alabama with y'all this year."

"I hope everything turns out alright for you and just keep me informed. I understand if you can't come, but if things turn around, we'll head out from Greenville tomorrow at 6 a.m."

"Thanks, and I'll keep updating you on what's going on."

"Hey Shane, thanks for coming."

"Not a problem. We grabbed a bite to eat

and was wanting to see how she was."

"You got here just in time. Visiting hours are in just a few minutes at 8:15."

"How are y'all holding up?"

"It's been a long day. Haven't eaten anything at all today. So much stuff to process! So many question! They try to explain everything to us, but it's overwhelming and feels so surreal. We better get in line so when they open the doors we are able to see her for a few minutes."

"How long can you stay back there?"

"Only fifteen minutes and only two people at a time."

"How's she doing, Jennifer?"

"We've gotten her stabilized. Not much change in the past few hours. She doesn't seem to be getting any worse, but she isn't showing any signs of improvement either. We did assess her a few minutes ago, and she still has movement in all her extremities. However, she still isn't responding to light."

"Thanks for the update. I'll go out so someone else can come in for a few minutes."

"I appreciate it Shane. I'm going to stay for a little longer. Hey Emily, I appreciate you coming up. It's been a hard day."

"I know it has. She doesn't look bad."

"I know; that's the crazy thing! How can she be in that bad of shape when she looks that healthy? She's got to be alright; I don't know what I'll do without her! She's more than just a

sister…she's one of my best friends. When I need someone to call, I'd always call her. Susan always knows how to cheer me up when I'm having a bad day, or give me advice when I need it. Crazy to think; she's always the one I call for advice, and she always knows what I need to hear."

"No matter what happens, Nathan, everything is going to be alright. God is still in control."

"Visiting hours are over. If you need anything, just buzz for me. I'll be looking after Susan all night." Jennifer politely explained.

"Are y'all staying up here tonight?"

"I don't think so Shane. I've not had a shower yet, and we need to get some rest in our own beds so we can get back up here early tomorrow morning."

"Dad, I want to stay. I know there isn't anything I can do, but if there are any changes I want to be the first to know."

"Well, if they have any updates they will call us."

"I need to be here to look after my sister!"

"We'll be back as soon as we can."

"Whatever!!!" Seemed to take forever to get home that night. "That GPS is taking us all over the place. We aren't even on a main road anymore. Just cut it off Dad, I've been on these roads before and can get us home. Turn left Dad, now take another left. There's the highway, that'll take us back home."

Chapter 12. I'd Rather Be At Church

We got home around 10 p.m. I got on Facebook to let everyone know about the incident and have them pray. Our family had always been very religious, but I'd never felt the need to pray as strongly as I did then. I didn't realize how many prayers I would need or how many people truly cared. I already had many comments on my Facebook page, and lots of people were expressing their concerns. Word sure spreads fast, especially in a small town. I lay in bed and began to pray. This was the hardest I had ever prayed! I prayed so much I must have dozed off.

I heard the phone ring. What time was it? It must still be very early…it was still dark outside. It barely rang once, and I answered it. Obviously, I wasn't in a deep sleep. I didn't even sound groggy when I anxiously answered, "Hello." I knew it had to be the hospital, and I knew by them calling so early it must be bad. I glanced at the clock, 4:33.

"This is Amber from Missions Memorial…we have the results of Susan's second CAT scan. You need to get up here as quickly as possible."

I knew they were planning on doing another CAT scan at 4 a.m., but I was hoping it would be negative like the first was. I went downstairs and met Mom in the hallway. I

couldn't speak…we just hugged and cried. Dad was still in bed, but I could hear him stirring around. A few minutes passed and Dad was up. Within minutes we were on our way back to the dreaded Asheville. I had made this trip many times while in college, but these past two seemed so much longer.

By 6 a.m. we were back on the 5th floor. I buzzed for the nurse, and she immediately came out to talk to me. I didn't have to tell her who I was. By now, they all knew me. She quickly paged the doctor for him to go over the CAT scan with us. It seemed like it took forever for him to see us, but within an hour, there we were with the doctor sitting in 'our' room again hearing the results of Susan's second CAT scan.

"Mr. and Mrs. Cole, we've gotten the results of Susan's CAT scan. Unfortunately, it indicates she had four strokes on the right side of her brain. She also has considerable swelling on the brain. I'm not going to sugar coat it…she's a very sick little girl. Best case scenario, she'll have months of rehab to even live a moderately normal life. She will never be the same Susan as you once knew. If she survives; she will have major disabilities."

"She will survive!?"

"I can't say that for sure, Nathan. She's been in a very traumatic accident and has numerous life-threatening injuries."

"Was she wearing a helmet?"

"I also can't definitively say that, but all

indications show she was."

"If she had on a helmet, how is her brain so messed up?"

"When you are in an automobile accident, your head is jarred. She hit with so much force her brain literally shook inside her head causing significant head trauma. I know this is a lot to process, but I just wanted to be completely honest with you. I'll let you take all this in and will let you know when I have further updates."

I waited till around 8 to call Stephanie; I knew she needed her sleep. I called, and Nelson answered. I didn't want to alarm Stephanie until they arrived, but I emphatically told Nelson they needed to come on up…it wasn't looking good. By this time, Jesse's family were at the hospital. They ended up having to airlift him to Missions Memorial as well. He had a cracked skull and a shattered left arm. He also was in the ICU neuro-trauma unit and had to have emergency brain surgery. The surgeon had to remove several skull fragments on his brain. Between his family and mine, we had a room full of people.

"Hey Nelson, where's Stephanie?"

"She's coming. She's having a real hard time dealing with this whole situation."

"I know. It doesn't seem real. I keep telling myself it's a dream and I'll eventually wake up. She only has a couple cracked ribs and very little outwardly damage…how can she be so bad?" That was the question we kept asking ourselves and the question that was so difficult to

comprehend.

Shortly after Stephanie and Nelson arrived, Shane called to get an update. He wanted to let the congregation know how Susan was doing. He was just at the hospital the night before, but things had taken a dramatic turn for the worse the past twelve hours. I let Shane know it wasn't looking good at all for her, and he assured me they would have a special prayer for her and our family. I certainly could feel those prayers and definitely needed them. I questioned if he still believed in miracles. I was desperately begging God for one now.

Seemed kind of strange not being at church this morning. However, I wouldn't have been able to pay attention anyways; my mind was certainly somewhere else. By 1 p.m., the waiting room was slam full of people once again. I knew people cared for us, but never comprehended this kind of outpouring from my extended family and friends. By 4 p.m., I had already received hundreds of calls, texts, and emails from people sending their best wishes and ensuring me they would pray. And pray they did!

It was time for us to meet with the doctor again. I now knew what Tim McGraw was thinking in his song, "Live Like You Were Dying," where he sings, "I spent most of my next days staring at the X-rays." I asked Dr. Thompson if we should consider surgery on her internal organs. He informed me right now her brain was their top priority and main focus.

"We've stabilized her internal organs, and

we'll worry about them when the time comes. I would like you meet Dr. Pikus. He is going to explain to you a device we can place in Susan's skull to monitor fluid on the brain."

"Nice to meet all of you. Like Dr. Thompson said, we can place a shunt on Susan's brain that can monitor her brain pressure and release fluid when necessary."

Dad further implored, "What are the advantages of this procedure?"

"Well, without it there is no way for us to know how much pressure is on the brain and no way to relieve any of this pressure. By aggressively pursuing any means necessary, we will have a better chance of saving her life."

"Is there any risk this could cause more damage to her?"

"There's always a small risk with any surgery, but it's a simple procedure that only takes about fifteen minutes. This is a great tool in managing the pressure on her brain."

"What does everyone think?"

"Well Dad, I definitely think we need to do whatever we can to give Susan the best chance of survival."

"I agree, but I don't want to perform an unnecessary surgery if it isn't going to help. I just don't want her to be cut up."

"I totally understand your concerns Mr. Cole, but this will only be a small hole in the top of her scalp, and her hair will cover the scar up. We will need to act quickly though…the longer we wait, the worse she'll get. Nurse, why is her

body temperature below 92 degrees?"

"We placed ice pads on her body to put her in a hypothermic state which will lower her body temperature. This will help reduce the level of oxygen she needs for her brain."

"I fully understand the procedure, but I've never performed this surgery on anyone whose body temperature was below 94. Go ahead and take her off the ice pads. Once her temperature increases to the right degree, I will prep her for surgery."

Shane was in the waiting room with many other people. By this time, we had overflowed to two waiting rooms. I went out and informed everyone we had decided to place a device in her head to monitor the pressure and fluid on her brain. "They will have to wait until her body temperature increases to 94 to begin. This will allow them to not only monitor her pressure, but also release a little fluid off the brain."

A couple of Susan's friends, Stephanie and Michelle, came by to see her. It was visiting time again so I let them go in to see Susan. After a few minutes, they came out. Michelle was bawling and asked the question we were all thinking, "How can she be so bad?" She frantically told me she had tried calling Susan all day yesterday and was unable to reach her. She insisted it wasn't like her not to return a call. Stephanie gave me a bookmark with an angel pin on it and simply told me to give it to Susan when she got better. I hoped and prayed I could one day give this bookmark to Susan. It was hard to

be strong and comfort her friends when we were hurting just as bad. Everyone decided we needed to try to eat something. I wasn't hungry at all but followed the crowd to the cafeteria.

I rode in the elevator with Shane and pleaded, "Is Susan going to be alright?"

He politely responded, "I don't know Nathan, it looks pretty bad. She may not make it."

Once again my eyes filled up with tears. I knew it was bad; I just wanted someone to tell me otherwise. It must have took half an hour for all of us to get through the line. I grabbed a burger and a juice, went through the checkout, and sat down. I didn't really remember eating or how it tasted, but when Lois wondered how the burger was I responded, "Luscious!"

Lois brought us all some toothpaste and toothbrushes. Seemed like such a small gesture, but it was the small things we forget to do that reminded us how much people truly cared. A couple hours passed, and Dr. Pikus informed us it was time to perform the procedure. He assured us there was nothing to worry about, and it would only take around fifteen minutes. True to his word, around fifteen minutes later Dr. Pikus came out and said the device went in smoothly. "We are beginning to monitor the pressure activity on Susan's brain. Her ICP was at thirty-six initially, and we have reduced it down to under thirty. This is obviously still high but should reduce more shortly. Typically, it is higher immediately after surgery. We will put

the ice pads back on her and begin slowly decreasing her body temperature to 91 degrees. This should also help with the pressure on her brain since less oxygen will be needed to pump the blood through the body."

I bet there were a hundred people that came by to speak with us, send their best wishes, and see Susan today. Among these were Michelle Arrowood, Susan's childhood friend. Well, I guess it ain't Arrowood anymore since she got married yesterday. I met her and her Mom in the elevator as we were going to the cafeteria once again. I don't know why I kept going to the cafeteria; it ain't like I was going to be able to eat anything. I went back to the waiting room with them, and we talked for a while. This was the wedding Susan and Jesse had came down to see yesterday. This was the wedding they never made it to. Fortunately, she had not heard about the wreck until after her wedding. I was so glad for that. Her husband was away on business, and they would go on their honeymoon later. Susan always had great friends and made a positive impression on everyone she came in contact with. No one ever had a bad thing to say about Susan, and everyone loved spending time with her.

I assumed it was time to let everyone know we would be unable to go to work for a few days. I don't really know how I found everyone's phone number I needed to contact, but things like that seem to always fall into place.

"Mr. Grimmer, this is Nathan Cole,

Susan's brother. Susan has been in a very bad motorcycle wreck and will not be at school for the rest of the year. I'll be in touch with Miss Watts on any updates."

"Thank you, and tell the family I send my best regards."

"Mr. Rogers, this is Nathan Cole, Barbara's son. I wanted to let you know my sister, Susan, has been in a very bad motorcycle wreck. My mom will be out of school for at least a week."

"Tell her to take as long as she needs, and we can cover her classes the rest of the semester if needed."

"Thanks a lot, I'll be in touch."

I must have talked to hundreds of people today. I tried getting in touch with Neil, our old youth pastor, but could only reach his voice mail. I left a couple of messages with him hoping and praying he would return my call soon. He seemed to always have the right words to say to make me feel better. Greg and Winters had been at the hospital most of the day comforting me. I called Ashley and gave her the bad news. She was in Florida but assured me everything was going to be alright, and she would be by tomorrow to see me. She wouldn't be the only one to come by, but she was the one I needed most for some reason.

The later and later it got, the fewer and fewer people remained. Eventually, once again it was just me, Mom, and Dad. Shortly there after,

an elderly lady entered the room. She let us know her name was Nancy, and the hospital had called her just for our family. She explained she was one of the chaplains at the hospital and assisted with families dealing with a traumatic event. She was a very nice lady, and I knew she meant well, but I saw her as the 'Grim Reaper.' I asked her if she was there because Susan was going to die. She assuredly said no; she only wanted to help in this difficult time. I didn't believe her. I knew she was the 'Grim Reaper.' She wanted to know about Susan. Mom and Dad shared stories about what kind of person Susan was.

Why were they talking like she was dead? She wasn't dead…she would get better! Stop talking in past tense! I couldn't listen to this! I tuned her out! I emphatically told her I wanted a pillow! I don't know why; I couldn't sleep. She brought us three and acted as if she could barely get that many. She left saying she would be back soon. In a way she was comforting, but it was that eerie kind of comfort I didn't like. I buzzed for the nurse. With tears in my eyes, I asked a question. She politely answered which comforted me for a moment. Five minutes later, I thought of another question; I buzzed again. The nurse promptly came out. I couldn't sleep. I buzzed again. "Can I go see my sister please?" I walked in her room all by myself. I knew it was bad and so did the nurses. They let me visit as long as I needed. It wasn't visiting hours, but they didn't seem to mind. I stayed for about ten

minutes and kindly thanked the nurses, nodded my head, and went back to the waiting room. A few minutes passed, I had another question. Buzz, buzz, buzz. "Can I see the nurse?"

"Just a moment, Nathan."

It's bad when the entire nursing staff knew my name. "Any improvements with my sister?"

"I'm sorry, Nathan, but she's about the same."

Have you tried this? Have you tried that? I'm no doctor, but I wanted to help my sister. The nurses kindly listened to my suggestions and assured me they were doing all they could. I must have dozed off. I couldn't believe I hadn't thought of that! Buzz, buzz, buzz. "I need to see the nurse please." I asked several more questions and gave many more suggestions. I've got to figure out how to save my sister. Once again, I sanitized my hands and went back to see Susan. I desperately wanted to stay by her side as long as I could. The nurse came in and checked on her once again. I thought of everything imaginable to ask the nurse and comfortable with her answers eventually went back to the waiting room. A few minutes passed while scenarios ran through my mind. I've got it! Buzz, buzz, buzz. All choked up, I buzzed for the nurse again. Do you think this would work? Have you tried this or that?

Chapter 13. Another Sleepless Night

It was a little after 4 a.m., and I heard a noise. I woke up from my sleepless slumber and saw them rolling my sister down the hall. I ran to the hallway and emphatically asked, "Where are you taking my sister?"

"She's taken a turn for the worse, and we're sending her for another CAT scan."

Worse? Worse? How was that even possible, I thought to myself?

My parents woke up shortly after 6 and wanted to eat some breakfast. Eat? How could you think about food at a time like this? I declined the offer saying I wanted to stay near Susan. They went down to the cafeteria. I then realized, I was all alone for the first time since the incident and didn't know what to do. I felt helpless. Not thinking of the time, I called Winters. I couldn't reach him. I was freaking out! Had something happened to him too? I didn't know what to do. I called his other number. I couldn't reach him. I called Julia. Again, no answer. I called his parents completely hysterical. His dad answered. Panicked, I told him I couldn't reach Winters, and I needed to talk to him. He assured me he was probably just asleep and informed me it was still 6:30 in the morning. I didn't care; I had to talk to someone. I called Greg. He answered. I told him my parents had went to eat breakfast,

and I was all alone. I didn't like being alone. He talked to me for a while and was able to calm me down. Finally, Mom and Dad were back.

Jesse was no longer in ICU, but his family stayed with us most of the day. I asked how he was doing, trying to be polite. They let me know he was having pretty severe headaches, and the doctors were planning on performing surgery on his elbow later that week. His dad kept saying I needed to go down and move her jeep. Why was this on his mind now? I had way more important things to worry about then where Susan's jeep was parked. Dr. LeeCock came by to introduce himself to the family. He was a very polite and large man. I could see true concern in his face, which was comforting. He informed us they were going to reassess Susan's injuries and would give us an update shortly.

Shane had came back up to visit today. Emily was at work, so Kenny came with him. They had just arrived when the doctor came in to give us the update. Shane offered to wait outside but we all insisted he stay. "After all, you're family too!"

"Hello everyone, we've gotten the results back from Susan's third CAT scan and unfortunately the images aren't encouraging. Not only does her right hemisphere show significant damage; her left hemisphere is also showing signs of swelling and brain damage. This morning we assessed the movement of all her limbs, and she had no movement at all. She didn't even have reflex movement; meaning,

when we tapped her knees and elbows she didn't have a jerk reaction. This indicates significant brain damage that is often irreversible. However, just a moment ago we reassessed her, and she was moving three of the four extremities. Although she does have significant head injuries, she is not what we classify as brain dead."

I was looking for anything to hold on to as a glimmer of hope. This slight encouraging word was what I used to revive me. I went by Jesse's room today and optimistically told him and his family the 'good news.' They ecstatically said, "That's great…keep the good news coming."

Shane and Kenny took me out to eat lunch. I hadn't eaten much in the past three days. I didn't really want to eat now; I just wanted to get a belt to help keep my pants up. Therefore, they took me shopping and got me out of the hospital for a while. They took me to T.G.I. Friday's where I finally ate. It was only a sandwich, but that was more than I'd had for a while. We then went by K-Mart and picked up a belt. Shane bought some gum and offered me a piece, but I didn't want one. It was nice to get away for a while, and they knew that would do me some good.

Finally, Ashley arrived at the hospital. I was so glad to see her. It was refreshing having her there with me. I cared about her more than even I would ever admit. We went in to see Susan for a few moments. She had never met

Susan before. Terrible way for a first encounter! She looked so peaceful, yet was in such grim shape. Ashley insisted she was going to be alright. I wanted to believe her…I wanted to believe her more than anything. Although others have said the same thing, her words tended to comfort me. I tried not to think…what if she's wrong! I tried not to think…what if she ain't alright! However, I'd be lying if I said that thought hadn't crossed my mind. Just having Ashley with me comforted me. Kind of strange, Winters and Greg have been with me the whole time, but there was just something special about Ashley. We walked around the hospital for a while. We decided to stop by and see how Jesse was doing. Although I'd been to his room once before, I didn't exactly remember how to get there. Eventually, I saw Stephen sitting in another waiting room. So many waiting rooms! So much time to sit and think! I inquired where Jesse's room was. He pointed, "Right down there." Rhonda was there and so was his mom and brothers. We asked how they were doing? They lied and said 'fine.' Fine…such a generic way to express yourself. No one ever says how they truly feel. Why does everyone use that word when it was obvious things were far from 'fine'?

Chapter 14. Can We Catch A Break?

After receiving what I took as 'good news,' we chose to go home for the night. We debated whether to go home or not. I definitely wanted to stay as close to Susan as I could in case anything developed. However, Dad insisted we go home, shower off, and sleep in our own beds. We asked the nurse what she thought, and she said she couldn't make that decision for us. She told us if anything developed they would call us immediately. After a few minutes of debating back and forth, we headed home for the evening.

We arrived home around 10 p.m. I got back on Facebook to update everyone on Susan's condition. There were hundreds of comments to go through. I couldn't respond to even a fraction of them, but it was nice to know so many people cared. After about an hour on Facebook, I went to bed. Of course, it was another restless night. I just had way too many things on my mind to ever fall asleep. I managed to get a few minutes of sleep here and there. Shortly after 6 the next morning, the phone rang once again. You always know it's bad news when the phone rings this early. It was the hospital again. They informed me it was just a matter of time before Susan would no longer be with us. I hung up the phone and began to cry. This was the first time I let it sink in I must spend the rest of my life without my sister…without my best friend. I tried the

best I could to gather myself. I called Greg asking if he could drive us to the hospital. I knew it wouldn't be a good idea for my dad to drive. He arrived at my house shortly to take us to the hospital. We didn't say much the entire way up. We were all thinking the same thing.

We arrived at the hospital a little after 7, and the doctor was ready to give us the grim news. We stated we wanted to wait until Stephanie and Nelson arrived. They would be here shortly. For the next couple of hours, we all just sat there waiting for the inevitably bad news. Just sitting there silently waiting was torturous, knowing everything was out of our control. It was all in God's hands now. It always is, always was, and always will be.

Around 9, Stephanie and Nelson arrived at the hospital. Obviously, we all wanted to be somewhere else, anywhere else. Unfortunately, on this particular day, the hospital was where we had to be. Dr. LeeCock came back in the room we had gathered, shut the door, and sadly began giving us the report. "As you all know, Susan is a very sick little girl." Funny, she was twenty-seven years old, and they always referred to her as a little girl. In retrospect, she was entirely too young to be there, too young to be clinging to life. He went on to say, "she's showing virtually no movement in her extremities and is not responding to light. She is not in what we refer to as a vegetative state; however, she is not showing any signs of improvement. As a family, you need to begin thinking about arrangements."

Arrangements, what does he mean? How could there be nothing left for them to do? I had to think of something…I had to save my sister. Even though I knew it was too late, I wasn't going to stop trying. I tried to think of every question imaginable, and the doctors politely answered every question and concern I had, despite how ridiculous some of them inevitably were. I even asked if they could perform a brain transplant. Obviously, that is impossible and ridiculous, but if it was your sister clinging to life wouldn't you ask for a miracle as well?

I heard Shane on the phone. He quietly told the person on the other line I was devastated. Devastated…that was the word he used and what an appropriate one at that. I could barely move. It was hard to imagine this much pain and hurt, yet still be physically alive. I could hardly function. I didn't know how I could possibly go on living knowing my sister soon wouldn't be. Could a person ever self-destruct from grief?

This whole experience had been so surreal. Surreal…that was a word I'd rarely heard before, but became an all too familiar term on the 5th floor. Very few people truly experience a surreal moment in their lives, but there we were living in a surreal world. It must have been visiting hours again because the lines were beginning to form. I guess the lines didn't affect myself; the nurses would let me see my sister anytime I felt the need. I saw a man whose wife was in a four-wheeling accident. We nodded at each other, knowing what we were

both dealing with. I asked how she was, and he responded positively. He cheerfully said she may get out of ICU by the end of the week. I was happy for him but sad for myself. My eyes filled with tears once again because I knew I would not be walking these halls by the end of the week either.

Six people were in our unit…four with major head trauma due to motorcycles or ATVs. Yet people still ride them, despite the risks. How can it not even be a law in South Carolina to wear a helmet? Do they want people to die? Do they want to put people through what we've been put through? Tell them to visit the 5th floor…they'll change their mind…they'll change the law.

I was glad they were so many people that came by, so many people that put their lives on hold to step a foot in our lives. I knew it affected them too, but what were they thinking? What was running through their minds? The entire family had been there throughout this ordeal. Wow…there were so many people. Our two waiting rooms now have filled a third room and spilled into the hallway. It helped pass the time…a friendly face, a compassionate word. My phone rang. It rang again and again and again. I tried to answer without getting choked up. I shared Susan's fate to everyone who called and begged each one to continue to pray. Funny to think, so many people cared. Crazy to imagine how many lives Susan affected. I was so glad Ashley had stopped back by today. Stephanie

had Nelson, Mom and Dad had each other, but I had no one.

Ashley stayed with me for several hours today and reassured me she would be back tomorrow. With all the things I wasn't looking forward to, having her stop by was one thing I was. Greg asked if I wanted to get something to eat. I told him I wasn't hungry; I couldn't eat at a time like this. He responded by saying, "Well lets go out to the car for a little while and try to clear your head. You need some fresh air and you need to get off the 5th floor."

How could you clear someone's head who had so many things running through it? How could anyone possibly take my mind off what was going on right now? I must admit, it was nice to get off the 5th floor for a few moments. We walked outside, and I saw a butterfly. Amazing, black with just a little purple on its wings. Was that a sign? Was God trying to tell me everything was going to be alright? I stared at the butterfly for several minutes. It was strange, but I felt at peace. The butterfly fluttered away in the cool night air. Me and Greg sat in the car for over an hour talking. I had so many things running through my mind, so many unanswered questions.

Eventually, we went back in the hospital and back to the dreaded 5th floor. It was supper time now, and the halls were still slam packed with visitors. There were other patients, but by far, most of the visitors were there to see Susan. A few would share stories about the kind of

person she was; some would tell of trips they had been on with her; several would let us know how she always made time for them, and others would simply be there supporting us. Regardless of why so many people came to the 5th floor, they were all there for one reason…they loved Susan!

The nurse came out to see us and said we needed to go in to say our final farewells to Susan. Final farewells!? What do you say to someone you would never see again? How could you tell them how much you loved them and what they meant to you? Two by two people began going into Susan's room. Two by two people came out. What were they saying? I didn't know what to say. I was not just losing a sister…I was losing a best friend, a confidant. I felt like I was losing my twin. I was told it was my time to go in; it was my time to say my final farewells. I couldn't! I collapsed. I couldn't stand up. Shane lifted me up. "I'll go in with you, Nathan." I walked past the nurses once again barely able to move. I stopped and began bawling. I didn't want to go see her. I didn't want to admit this would be the last time I would ever see my sister. I finally made it to her room. I stood over her crying. Nurse Matt insisted I could hold her hand if I wanted. I did. Could she feel me? I squeezed and begged her to squeeze back. I couldn't tell if she did. I hoped she was. I stayed in there for a while. Now I didn't want to leave. If I left I may never see her again. Leaving would be admitting she was gone. I couldn't admit that. Not now! Not ever! I

stayed a while longer. Shane left me alone for a while. I couldn't muster up any words to say. I couldn't speak; my throat had a huge lump in it. Did she know I loved her? Did she know I would have gladly taken her place? Did she realize there wasn't anything I wouldn't do for her? Why could I not find the words to tell her how much I cared?

Visiting hours were over once again. The hallways began clearing out. Only a few people remained. Greg was still there. After all, he had driven us up this morning expecting the inevitable to be over by now. Against all odds, she was still clinging to life. How was that possible with all her life-threatening injuries? Of course, we all knew without a miracle she wouldn't be able to cling much longer. Greg called his wife and explained to her he was staying at the hospital tonight. This was the first time he had spent a night away from her. They had only been married six months. I was glad he was staying tonight. I knew this would be a very, very long evening.

Chapter 15. 18 Minutes

The waiting room was beginning to fill up again. It was around 9 a.m. and the nurse questioned whether anyone wanted to see Susan one last time. Forest and Doris said they would like to since they were unable to the day before. They went in for a few minutes and came out with tears in their eyes. Mom, Dad, and I then decided we would like to see her one last time as well. This was a decision I would soon regret. This was an image I could only pray would not remain etched on my mind. I adamantly told Stephanie not to go back in. I sadly told her, that wasn't Susan lying in that morbid hospital bed. She let me know she had spoken her final regards to Susan the night before. She informed me everything she needed to say was said last night. I was glad for that. I wished I had said all I wanted to. How could you say anything and then again how could you say nothing? I desperately hoped she knew how I felt!

After everyone had a chance to see her, the doctors inquired about Susan's wishes regarding organ donation. We had no idea! I mean, who discusses things like that! No one ever expects to be in this situation! Since she had not indicated on her license, it was our decision to make. After careful consideration, we determined we wanted her organs to be used to help other people. At this time, the doctors informed us they must warm her body

temperature to 98 degrees before they could remove her organs. They informed us this procedure could take another three to four days. Wow…we were going to have to wait this much longer before Susan was technically gone. As if we hadn't been through enough already.

"After reassessing Susan's injuries, we have determined the only organ that could potentially help someone else is her right kidney. There is only a 50-50 chance this organ hasn't been damaged beyond functional use. We can attempt to save this organ if you would like, but again it's going to take at least seventy-two hours to get her body temperature back up."

Dad replied, "I don't believe it's worth it just for one organ that may not be usable." We all agreed we had been through enough and another few days of waiting would be unbearable.

"That's your decision. I'm now going to let you speak with a member from the Lions Club about donating her eyes."

"Hello everyone, I'm Mike from the local Lions Club and was wanting to see if you had given any thought to donating Susan's eyes." My Dad immediately spoke up. He was also in the Lions Club and would love for Susan's eyes to restore sight to someone else. No one had any objections, so Mike consulted with the doctors about this decision. Unfortunately, her eyes had been infected with a disease and were no longer functional. Wow…how many ailments can one person have, I thought to myself? Even her eyes

had been damaged during this tragic accident.

Since none of Susan's organs were functional for transplants, Myrca, another one of the hospital chaplains, came back in to speak with us.

"Does anyone want to go back in to see Susan, be in the room during the transition stage, or see her after she passes?"

Of course I didn't want to be in the room during this time, and no one else did either.

"Well, what will happen now is all the machines will be turned off, we will take her off the respirator, and she will peacefully pass away."

My Dad tearfully asked, "How long will this take?"

Myrca politely responded, "It will only take a few moments and she won't feel a thing." She then said, "I will tell the nurses to begin the process." It was 10:35 a.m. How long can one last without any medical help? 18 minutes! At 10:53 a.m. on Wednesday April 22nd Susan went on to be with the Lord.

Chapter 16. Planning The Funeral

Gregg, our family deacon, called and I struggled to find the words to tell him Susan was gone. He kept asking me to repeat myself; he simply couldn't understand through my choked up words. I couldn't bear telling him she was dead. I couldn't speak without a huge lump in my throat or tears streaming down my face. I felt paralyzed, unable to move, and barely able to speak.

How could I possibly tell the hundreds of people that would call that my sister was dead? How would they possibly react or be able to even remotely fathom what I was dealing with? He asked if we wanted him and Kenny to cut our grass. Funny question I thought, but I mumbled, "Sure." I called Wesley asking if he would charge Susan's phone and shut her door. We stayed at the hospital for another hour speaking with Myrca and talking with family and friends. Myrca wanted to know all about how Susan was. It was so incredibly difficult for me to think about Susan in the past tense.

Ashley arrived at the hospital shortly before we left. I hugged her and tearfully told her the bad news. Obviously, this was the worst news I had ever had to share with anyone. She told me how sorry she was, and I believed her.

We got home around 1 p.m., and there were so many people already at our house. Gregg and Kenny had just finished cutting the

yard. Rhonda, Lois, and Mary were cleaning the house. We needed to go through Susan's purse so we could find her keys. Brandon helped me search through it. We located many items but were unable to locate her keys. We found the ticket to the National Championship game she had attended just a couple weeks earlier. We had so much food to eat, and so many people were visiting. The rest of the day and throughout the evening, people stopped by to send their condolences.

The medical examiner called me early the next morning and went over his findings. After I heard this news, I had to get out of the house. I called Matt to see if I could come over. He had worked third shift the night before but allowed me to come visit for a while. I figured he would have some good advice since he was a cop. I went by and talked to him about what all the medical examiner revealed to me. We drove to The Drop In where his wife, Michelle, worked. She hugged me and truthfully told me how sorry she was. She informed me they would be unable to make it to the funeral, because they were going on vacation. I knew there would be tons of people at the funeral and understood they had prior arrangements. Matt asked if I wanted a pizza to eat, and I told him I wasn't hungry. After all, we had enough food at home to feed a small army.

Shortly there after, it was time to meet with the funeral home director. There were still a ton of people at the house, so we let them make

themselves at home. Susan's good friend, Cassandra, stopped by just before we left and brought a flower in a smiley face mug. Susan always had a smile on her face and loved anything with a smiley face, even had a smiley face tire cover on her jeep. We told Cassandra to eat some food and for her to make herself at home as well. The funeral home was just up the street, and we arrived within a few minutes.

There were so many decisions we had to make in such a short time frame. What did we want the obituary to say? Had we considered a memorial fund? Had we picked out a burial plot? Had we decided on a florist? What casket would we like? Whom did we want as pallbearers? Whom did we want to perform the ceremony? Had we thought about singers or musicians? Which songs would we like sung? Had we thought about what we wanted her to be buried in? Wow…this was overwhelming! People take months to plan a wedding, and we were expected to plan a funeral in forty-eight hours. At least planning a wedding is a joyous time. It was so hard to plan Susan's funeral, but I had to make every detail perfect for her. It was a strange thought, but at times it felt like I was planning my own funeral. I knew if it had been me killed and not her many of the details involved in planning my funeral would have been similar. I kept thinking, what would I want when I die, and I knew Susan would have wanted the same. We were so much alike in so many different ways. Although emotionally I may have died,

physically it wasn't me no longer with us.

After careful consideration we wrote a collaborative obituary.

> "Susan Elizabeth Cole, age 27, of Gastonia, died Wednesday, April 22, 2009 at Memorial Mission Hospital in Asheville. Susan was born October 25, 1981 in Rutherford County to Jimmy and Barbara Cole. She was a teacher in the More at Four program at Forest Heights Elementary in Gastonia. She was a special person with a love for children and her family. She was a member of the Chase High School Class of 2000 and also a 2004 graduate of the University of North Carolina-Greensboro. She was a member of Floyd's Creek Baptist Church. She was preceded in death by her grandfather, James Scruggs and grandparents, Euell and Jeanette Cole. In addition to her parents she is survived by her sister, Stephanie Long and her husband, Nelson of Rutherfordton; her brother, Nathan Cole of Forest City; her fiancé, Jesse of Gastonia, her grandmother, Lorena Scruggs of Forest City and several Aunts, Uncles, and cousins."

After writing the obituary, Lanny took us all in a closed off room to pick out a casket. We looked at a number of different ones. We saw

your basic silver caskets, and we saw your flamboyant caskets. We joked about getting a casket that had a drawer where you could pull out and see her anytime you wanted. Funny thing, Susan always joked that was the kind of casket she wanted. Obviously, they don't make those kind of caskets. However, it would be nice to be able to see her anytime we wanted. It would be wonderful if we could still see her and talk with her whenever we felt the need. We finally chose a light purplish casket with a dove on the inside.

After picking out the casket, we went to the florist to pick out flowers to place on Susan's grave. We picked out many purple ones, Susan's favorite color. Each of us picked out several flowers we thought would be appropriate and had the florist make the arrangement. I then contacted Mr. Grimmer about a memorial fund in memory of Susan. He reaffirmed that would be a great gesture. I made sure all the money would be used for playground equipment for the school and funds for her children to go on field trips. I truthfully told him she always loved going on field trips with her students.

The night before, we had gone to the church with Stephen to pick out a burial plot. We chose a spot down by the road and went ahead and reserved three more, one for myself, Mom, and Dad. It's kind of morbid to already have a burial plot picked out. However, if anything happens to me, I want to be close to Susan. After all, Susan hadn't expected to need a burial plot either.

We all carefully decided who we wanted as pallbearers. We knew we wanted Timothy to play the organ. Wesley, Jamie, Andrew, and Brandon were four obvious pallbearers. We debated back and forth about whether to ask Cody and Nick, Jesse's brothers, to be the final two pallbearers. However, we needed them to bring us some of Susan's dresses so we could choose one for her to be buried in, and they never did. We waited until the last possible moment before finally deciding to choose Greg and Winters to be the final two pallbearers. As far as the dress, we went shopping at Belk's. Mom picked out the one Susan had looked at just a couple weeks earlier. This dress was purple and covered with butterflies. A butterfly is but a simple creature, yet such a peaceful one that will surround Susan's body from now on.

Lanny suggested us gather some pictures of Susan for the video that would be shown at the receiving of friends. It took us hours to go through all the ones we had gathered. It was nice looking through all the pictures from the past and remember all the good times we had together. However, it was also extremely tough reflecting on the kind of person she was…knowing we would never have the opportunity to make more pictures together. People so often take life for granted, until it's too late. It was so difficult limiting the pictures to place in the video. There were so many that not only reminded us of her but also brought out her unique personality. We finally chose about twenty we felt were the most

appropriate and took them and the clothes to the funeral home. I then contacted Joey about some music we could play at the funeral. Within an hour, he came over and helped me pick out some songs. I called Elora asking if she could sing a song. She was honored I thought of her as was Jolayne when I requested she play the piano. I called John and Rodney about singing "There will be a Day" by Jeremy Camp. They tried to learn it before the service, but unfortunately, they were unable to master it. We decided to just have this song play over the speaker system. We also decided we would have everyone sing "Jesus Loves Me" as people were filing in for the service. Susan loved teaching children, and in lots of ways she was still a child herself. I wanted to get musicians and speakers who meant something in Susan's life. Therefore, I contacted Neil, our first youth pastor, about helping Shane with the ceremony. He informed me he had a wedding at 2 but would be available by 4. Neil asked if there was anything special I wanted him to say.

I thought about it for a while, and I felt Amber summed it up best.

> "I remember Susan as a very bright person who was always smiling. She tried her best not to judge me even though I was a hard person to get to know in middle school and high school. I think that says a lot about the kind of person that you were. My thoughts go out to the family and hope they know that one of

God's angels... have been taken home.
God bless and rest in peace."

MORE AT FOUR TEACHER

Chapter 17. Final Farewells

It was time for the receiving of friends. Seemed like all we had been doing was meeting with family and friends. It was times like these when it was wonderful to have so many people who cared. However, we had one more major decision. Should we have an open or closed casket. We went back and forth on this issue for a while and were split in our final decision. Stephanie and myself wanted to have a closed casket; we didn't think Susan looked like herself. Adam, the mortician, told us he could work on her some more, but it wouldn't matter. Dad was adamant people would want to see her one last time and say their final farewells. He exclaimed, she just looked so beautiful…and she did. After some deliberation, we chose to leave the casket open. Lanny then allowed us to view the video before the crowds began to file in. It was a very moving video. I watched it twice, took a couple of deep breaths, and began preparing myself to greet the hundreds of people I knew I would come in contact with this evening.

There were tons of plants and flowers surrounding the casket. Ashley had sent some white carnations, which was very meaningful. People began filing in nearly an hour before the scheduled time. This was the moment I had dreaded all day. How would I be able to hold in my emotions? How would I make it through this night? What would I say to people? What would

they say to me? I saw Susan lying in the casket and couldn't help but think, "What if that were me lying there?" With all the people coming to see her, I felt like I was experiencing my own funeral. We were so alike it was uncanny! Hundreds of people came by to express their sympathies. Each one had a different story of how they knew Susan and how she had touched their lives. Mr. Grimmer came by and gave us a packet from the school. This packet had many cards from Susan's students. It was a joy reading these cards and learning just how much Susan was loved from all. I thought it was amazing how many of Susan's childhood friends came by to see her one last time. Brandy, Erin, and Michelle all came by. These were friends Susan had since kindergarten. Amy also came by. She was crying uncontrollably. I knew what she was feeling. I knew what was going through her mind. I urged her to call me anytime she needed because I had been there too…I had lost my best friend. People always support the family, but often forget the friends. They were hurting too; they had lost someone special as well. Many others came by that never knew Susan, just wanted to be there for the family. The hospital discharged Jesse so he would be able to come. He arrived in a wheelchair, neck brace, and arm sling. With help from his brothers, he leaned over Susan's casket, sadly told her he loved her, and cried hysterically. What must he be thinking? How bad must he be hurting? How bad were we all hurting!? Tonight wasn't as bad

as I had thought, hopefully I can say the same about the funeral tomorrow.

Saturday, April 25th, Granny's birthday. Just a week earlier my cousin, Christina, had celebrated her 18th birthday. Obviously, I had other things on my mind today, but their birthdays would now always be remembered other than just the day they were born. I woke up this morning and took about two hours to read all the comments on Facebook. There were so many people that had left loving comments about Susan. I loved hearing all the good things they had to say, but it made me sad knowing there would be no other good times with her.

It was now time to get ready for the funeral…the final farewell. I desperately wanted to have Susan's funeral tomorrow. Of course, as they say, 'tomorrow never comes.' I just wanted to prolong the inevitable. I felt like as long as the funeral hadn't come, she was not really gone. I didn't really have to say goodbye if tomorrow never comes. It still didn't feel like this was forever. I mean death is so permanent, and forever is so long. We couldn't have it on Granny's birthday, her special day. I wore my green suit for the funeral. Lanny had arrived to escort us to the church. We gathered in the gym, the overflow room for the funeral. They had a big projector for spectators to view the service. Neil prayed, and we walked into the church to the congregation singing "Jesus Loves Me."

The ushers sat the family on the front row. After the family had been seated, they

wheeled Jesse in and sat him beside my dad. Dad squeezed his hand and sincerely said, "I forgive you." Tears welled up in both of their eyes. After the congregation finished singing "Jesus Loves Me," Elora got up and sang "If You Could See Me Now." Joey then sung "What a Day" just before we had "There Will Be a Day" play throughout the church. Shane spoke a few words about Susan and sincerely told me this was the hardest funeral he ever had to do.

I don't remember too much about the service, I just kept thinking, "How could I possibly be burying my sister today?" However, I do remember the last thing Shane said, "Susie Q, we'll miss you!" If ever there were a truer statement. Neil commented on how Susan always had a smile on her face. It was rare you saw her frown, even though she could make a perfect frown face. Neil concluded by having the congregation once again sing "Jesus Loves Me" as we went to the graveside.

As I left the church, I saw my good friend, Melissa, sitting on the back row. It was hard to see everyone; there were so many people at the service. Within a few moments, we were all gathered by the graveside. Shane spoke a few more words before the pall bearers came by, hugged the family, and placed a rose on the casket. Before they placed Susan's casket in the ground, Amy placed a flower on it, threw her body across the casket, and began to cry uncontrollably once again.

After the service, I was totally surrounded

by family and friends. This helped me not get lost in my thoughts. I saw family and friends I hadn't seen in years. My college roommate, Blair, was there with his wife. She was expecting their first child. Once again, I looked around for Ashley. I desperately needed to see her. I desperately longed for her to comfort me once again. People kept grabbing me, hugging me, and telling me they were sorry. I saw Neil and his wife, Pam. He asked what I was doing on Monday. I explained we had to go through Susan's house in Gastonia. He responded by saying, "We need to play some golf soon and get your mind off things." I agreed and hesitantly told him to call me next week. I finally saw Ashley and let her know we were all going back to my house to eat supper. She replied, "That's family time." I emphatically told her there would be so many people that one more would be fine. I wanted her to spend time with me so she could keep my mind off what I was dealing with. I heard Luke say, "Susan's in Heaven now." Although he was a preschooler, I knew he was right, and I should find comfort in this, but it was still too soon to rejoice. It was still way too soon to think of her as an angel singing in God's choir.

We went back home for a while to give them time to prepare the graveside. Of course, we still had more food than any of us could ever eat. Once again, there were tons of people at the house. Lanny began bringing the flowers and plants over. It took two full van loads. We placed them all in the basement since there were

so many people still in the house. Hard to imagine, all these plants and flowers fit in the funeral home. All these flowers were for Susan. We all tried to eat a little before heading back to the graveside. After about an hour, we all loaded up in our vehicles to head back to the church. By this time, the graveside was covered with flowers. It was very pretty but in the same time very sad. Crayton began taking pictures, which I thought was quite unusual and a little morbid. The sky was growing darker, and we saw several butterflies playfully fluttering around Susan's grave. We stayed at the graveside until just after dark, then went home to try and get some sleep.

It had been a very tiring last week, and surprisingly, I was able to sleep well tonight. I don't know if I fell asleep or simply passed out from pure exhaustion. I guess eventually your body becomes so drained it forces you to get some sleep. Nevertheless, I was just glad to finally be able to sleep more than twenty minutes at a time.

Chapter 18. Back To Church

This Sunday morning would be quite different than the ones in the past. We got up the same time we did every Sunday, got dressed, ate breakfast, and headed to church. Sunday School was very different this particular morning. I remember the Alcorns and Flynns discussing the topic of love.

I rarely speak during Sunday School but found myself compelled to talk. I tearfully told them, "Love is when people you haven't seen in years come to a hospital room to console you. Love is when people put their lives on hold to be there when you need them. Love is when a friend literally picks you up after you hear your loved one isn't going to make it. Love is when a father tells the one who killed his daughter, 'I forgive you.' Love is when a family member remembers to bring you a tooth brush and is willing to clean your house. Love is when a friend stays with you in a hospital room instead of spending the night with his new bride. Love is when you have more messages on Facebook than you ever have time to respond to. Love is seeing someone hurting and truly hurting yourself. Love is wanting to do anything for someone to relieve a little of their pain. Love is just sitting in a room with someone and feeling their hurt. Love is putting others needs before your own. Love is listening to others and just being a shoulder to cry on." The Bible tells us in 1

Corinthians 13:4-8, "Love is patient, love is kind. It does not envy, it does not boast, it is not proud. It is not rude, it is not self-seeking, it is not easily angered, it keeps no record of wrongs. Love does not delight in evil but rejoices with the truth. It always protects, always trusts, always hopes, always perseveres. Love never fails." So many people look at love as what can this person do for me and not how can I be there for them. After this ordeal, I truly have gained a deeper appreciation on life and what love truly means.

So many people came up to us and told us they were thinking about us. I saw Travis at church this morning. He didn't speak a word, but we both nodded at each other. We have a common bond now, a bond we wish we didn't share. We are now in the same club, a club no one wants to be a part of. After church this morning, we were asked if we wanted to go out to eat for Granny's birthday. Why wouldn't we want to? We normally would take her out for her birthday. The entire family went to Georgio's down in Boiling Springs.

After lunch, we all went back to the funeral home. This time we were there for our cousin, Betty Lancaster. Several people came up to us trying to console us. They inquired about how we were doing and we replied, "As good as can be expected." I saw Michele and let her know how sorry I was for the loss of her mother, and she said she was sorry for my loss as well. I haven't lost a parent, but I felt her pain. It was eerie being back at the funeral home this soon.

I'll always remember this as the last place I saw Susan. This was the place I had to say my final farewells.

Chapter 19. Taking Care Of Business

It was Monday morning now, but I was not going to work like most Mondays. We were heading to Gastonia today to pick up some items from Susan's house. We all got to the house by mid-afternoon. Nelson and I adamantly told Mom and Dad we would meet them at the school shortly. We were afraid of what we may find and didn't want to put my parents through that. We began searching through the house. I didn't really know what we were looking for, but I wanted some memories of Susan. Nelson and I gathered up some pictures, annuals, dolls, and mail, then searched through some other items. We found the title to the motorcycle through all the mess and realized Jesse's insurance expired six days before the wreck. He should never have been driving the motorcycle this day. This wreck should have never happened!

After a few more moments of gathering some items, we headed to Susan's school to meet back up with my parents. I met Mr. Grimmer once again and he asked how I was doing. Obviously, we still weren't doing well. It takes much longer than this before things would be remotely normal again. Of course, things will never again be normal. I guess we will have to work on creating a new normal. Easier said than done!

The next day I decided to go back to

work. I checked the sales from the previous week and straightened up the store a little bit. I told Samantha and Kyra I was in no shape to wait on any customers today. They assured me, "That was fine…do what you need to do." Around 11 a.m., Mr. Henderson walked in the store. He was a very polite customer and a pastor at a local church. He came up to me and could obviously tell I was very distraught. He asked if he could pray with me and I accepted. I was very appreciative of customers like that…customers who truly cared. After a few more minutes of straightening, I decided to head home. I was in no shape to work all day and I knew my staff could run the store.

That evening I decided to shoot ball. I didn't really feel like playing, but I couldn't be by myself to get lost in my thoughts. I arrived at the church around 7 p.m. and saw a note stating they wouldn't be playing until 7:45. I decided not to wait and went over to Greg's for a few moments. Greg told me he was on his way to Teddy's, but I could come. Of course I did, it was better than being alone.

The next day I only worked until lunch time again. I still couldn't bring myself to work longer than that. However, Thursday was shipment day, and I decided it was time for me to get back into my normal routine. As I previously mentioned, life will never exactly be normal again.

For the next few weeks, we still had more food than we could ever eat. At least once a

week, people would bring us food, invite us to eat, or take us out for dinner. Cards were already beginning to pour in. We received hundreds of cards throughout the month of May. I had tons of people that came by the store and asked how I was doing. By being in the public, I had at least one person tell me how much they were thinking about me and my family daily for over a month. However, it seemed the only people I was truly able to get any comfort from during this time were those who were in my club, Susan's childhood friends, and Ashley.

Mother's Day was fast approaching and I had no idea what to get my mom. I wanted to get her something extra special, but I always did my shopping with Susan. Christina offered to help me go shopping for Mom this year, but it just wouldn't be the same. I finally decided to call Stephanie to help me pick out a present at the Christian Bookstore.

May was not only a comforting month for me since I still knew how much people cared, it was also a tough month for me. I had a constant reminder Susan was no longer in my life. So many people asked how my parents were doing, but only a few were interested in how I was holding up. I kept thinking, "How do you think they are doing…their baby girl had been tragically killed!" Why didn't they ask about me; did they not know I was hurting just as bad? Did they not realize I not only lost my sister…I lost my best friend? Could they not see I was hurting from my loss, as well as trying to deal with the

grief my parents were feeling?

Not only had this month been like a roller coaster for me, it had also been quite a blur. I guess I tried to block out as much as I could about this time of my life. Even the simplest of decisions became an ordeal. In the weeks that followed the incident, I became like a robot. I did what I was told to. When I was told to eat, I tried eating a little bit. When it was time to go to work, I made every attempt to do the best job possible. Once it became dark, I tried to get a decent nights sleep. Our family had to literally help each other do the simple, mundane things of life most people do without any thought or effort. We had so many people reaching out to our family; however, as the month came to an end so did the food, calls, cards, visits, sympathies, and outpouring of love and support.

It was difficult being the only child at home now. Even though Susan hadn't lived at home in years, it felt different now. It was strange to think I was now the youngest child. When people ask how many siblings I have…what am I supposed to say? Both my parents were having a very difficult time coping with the death of their baby girl, which was understandable. My mother did very little but sit drowning in her own thoughts. I tried to stay home with her as much as I could, but found it difficult to comfort her. I desperately wanted her to feel better…for us all to feel better. I felt like I had to take care of my momma.

My dad tried to engulf himself at work

and stay as busy as possible. I could also understand wanting to do whatever necessary to fill your mind with something other than this devastating tragedy. It was obvious my mother wanted to share her thoughts with someone, anyone. However, my dad struggled ever mentioning that day or the events that occurred there after. I enjoyed sharing my thoughts and listening to my mom's thoughts as well. Sometimes though, it just became too overwhelming. It was very difficult at times to counsel her when I was in need of counseling myself. In the same regards, I felt everyone around me was tired of hearing about my pain and the incident. After all, they have moved on and weren't engulfed with grief. I hope I was not coming off as a nuisance or bother to them, but I needed someone other than my mom to truly care about my well-being.

Now I take it upon myself to speak with the police about the incident. Officer Hamby was in charge of the case and I called him weekly trying to determine the cause of the wreck. There must be a reason they wrecked! I couldn't accept Jesse simply lost control of the motorcycle. I had heard so many different perspectives on what happened that tragic April afternoon. I had my own theories on what happened. I had talked to Matt about what the medical examiner revealed to me, but kept that information to myself for weeks. I didn't want to further upset my family. It was an unbearable weight I placed on myself. How could we have Susan's blood results back

immediately and it take so long to get Jesse's? I was told they had to send his blood results to Chapel Hill and it may take months to get any answers. I later found out in Rutherford County, EMS don't draw blood at the scene of an accident. By the time he would have his blood drawn, he had been sedated, which would have compromised his results. I had to get answers on what happened that day. Anything to make me feel better and come to grips with the incident. People don't just wreck for no reason! I knew they were riding with another couple and assumed they were racing. I figured he passed the other bike and glanced back to see where they were. He probably didn't see the curve until it was too late to regain control. I decided to ride up to the scene with Ashley to get a better understanding on what may have happened. We pulled over on the side of the road and saw a cross someone had placed in memory of Susan. I assumed that was where the incident occurred. I walked around to see if there were any signs of an accident. I saw no skid marks, glass, or debris. Just like Susan, even the scene of the accident had no signs of a tragic event. Susan always said she didn't want a cross placed on the road if she died that way. Funny thing to discuss if you ask me…but that's just how Susan was. I didn't mind the cross, actually thought it was a good gesture. Susan needs to be remembered and not forgotten. I've been able to go to the scene of the accident many times, yet can't bring myself to go to the grave. I can't even bring

myself to throw away the bag full of clothes she was wearing on the day of that tragic accident or pour out the drink I had when the doctor sadly told me she was gone.

I went by the police station to see if they had a completed police report yet. They informed me they were still gathering all pertinent information. They also let me know they had impounded the motorcycle to see if they could better determine the cause of such a horrific accident. I must see what was in that report. I contacted my police friend, Matt, again and begged him to stay on top of this case for me. I was convinced this accident could have been prevented. I was certain there were events over the past twelve hours that had a direct influence on what happened. I expressed my concerns to both Matt and Officer Hamby. They assured me they would continue to investigate. I certainly hoped so. It wasn't until I informed Office Hamby that Jesse's insurance had lapsed that he realized he was driving uninsured. I wanted this case to be top priority. I didn't want anything slipping through the cracks. I wasn't out for revenge…I just wanted justice to be served. I felt like if one does anything voluntarily or not that results in the death of someone else that person should take responsibilities for their own actions.

Over the next few weeks, I would fail to do simple things at work. My mind was always somewhere else, whether I was thinking about Susan, the incident, the circumstances, the police report, how my mother was, or just drifting off in

my own thoughts. A couple Mondays after the wreck, Melony called to see if I had gotten the weekly numbers calculated. I had been the manager for over seven years and compiled these figures every Monday, but for some reason I had failed to complete them on this particular day. I told her I was sorry, but I simply forgot. She completely understood and was compassionate; she had lost her sister in a wreck many years earlier and empathized with myself. Unlike most people who are only able to sympathize with our family, she truly was able to empathize. As she was well aware, I was now part of her morbid club.

June was nearing now, and so was the dreaded thirtieth birthday. I had anticipated and some what dreaded this birthday for nearly a year, but in retrospect, it didn't seem as significant now. With everything I had dealt with these past few weeks, I could care less about getting a year older. However, it was a monumental birthday and Stephanie decided to throw me a party at her house. I had to work all day on my actual birthday, shipment day once again. As a result, we decided to have my party on Friday. We invited all my family and friends. This was the first time we had all been together since the funeral. Emilee and Wesley were excited about their upcoming wedding and wanted to practice "Cotton Eye Joe." No one wanted to dance to it, so I decided to be the guinea pig. Emilee and I got out in the front yard and had a blast dancing to this song while

everyone else watched.

By the end of June, virtually no one spoke anything to us about the incident or ever commented about Susan. As I previously mentioned, we now belonged to a club. This was a club no one wanted to be a part of. It was the same club Travis, Brian, Leslie, and even my boss Melony became a part of a few years back. However, this was a club I found comfort in. I felt like only the members of this club truly knew what I was dealing with and earnestly cared about my well-being. Sure, I had lots of family and friends who tried to console me. They didn't really know what I was thinking though…they didn't really understand what I was going through. They certainly didn't know what to say to make me feel better. After a while, even the ones closest to me didn't want to hear about my troubles anymore. After all, they had worries, issues, and problems of their own. It was just so hard for me to accept that my family wasn't the only ones in life hurting. We weren't the only people with heartache. Their problems were just as real to them as ours were to us. For me, it seemed others' problems were trivial and insignificant to what I have had to deal with. It seemed like everyone thought we had an incurable disease and if they spoke to us about the incident or Susan they would be infested with this disease. Maybe they didn't want to speak to us about it because they were simply tired of hearing of our pain, and they had no idea what to do or say to help. We did have something no one

else wanted; however, what we had wasn't contagious. We still needed their love; we still needed to know they cared. It would be nice if they wouldn't avoid us like the plague and would still talk to us about Susan. I believed people expected us to be getting better by now. I mean, after all, it had been two months. Two short months and we were supposed to be better! Most people have milk in their fridge that's older than that, yet everything was expected to be back to normal for our family.

Chapter 20. Girl Of My Dreams

On the Sunday before my birthday, Ashley asked if I wanted to go out to eat and meet this girl. I honestly told her, I was in no shape to meet anyone or be much company. She insisted and since it was Ashley, I reluctantly agreed. I arrived at Legal Grounds shortly before they did. I saw her pull up and disgustingly told her I had to go back to Gastonia in the morning to get more of Susan's stuff. I elaborated by saying the last time my parents went down, the locks had been changed on them. Jesse's family explained to us we could get some more stuff out of the house, but they had to be present. Why would they have to be present for us to get items out of her house?

Not only was I meeting Ashley for dinner, but her friend Morgan and her children were there, along with Shannon. I didn't have much to say during dinner…had many other things on my mind. When the waitress brought the bill, I told Shannon I would get hers, but she declined the offer.

The rest of the evening, Ashley kept calling and asking if I was going to text Shannon. I confusingly responded, "I don't know; I barely said two words to her. What if she doesn't want me to text her? I don't even have her number. She probably doesn't want you giving me her number." Ashley kept insisting. I obviously have lots of trust and value in Ashley. I decided

not to contact Shannon that night, but since Ashley was so persistent, I would text Shannon the next day.

The next day I took off work to go by Susan's house and school. The school had planted a tree for Susan and had a memorial plaque for her as well. We got to Susan's house fairly early the next day. Jesse's entire family was sitting in the living room. It was obvious someone had cleaned up a little bit. The last time we were there it was completely filthy. It was very strange searching through Susan's stuff while his family was observing us. We felt like we were intruding on them. Why should we feel this way…it was her stuff and her house? We only stayed for about an hour, gathered up as much as we could without feeling too awkward, and left to go to her school. While heading for the school, I decided to text Shannon. I explained to her I was sorry I hadn't spoken much the evening before…I just had way too much stuff on my mind. She understood.

Shortly before 3 p.m., we arrived at Forrest Heights Elementary. Mr. Grimmer gave us a brief tour of the school and then took us to Susan's classroom. They had a bulletin board in the hallway with a picture of all the active teachers. Susan's picture was still hanging on the board. Mr. Grimmer took it down and handed it to us. He told Jesse to get better soon so he could help move some stuff around the school. After looking at Susan's room, we headed outside to look at the memorial plaque and tree. It was just

outside her classroom where all her students would be able to see it and have a shade when playing on the playground. It was a very warm day and we could hear the birds chirping in the distance. We watched as a couple of squirrels were chasing each other around the playground. In the distance I saw a couple of butterflies. It seemed all of God's creatures were enjoying this hot summer day, while we were still desperately mourning, desperately wishing we could turn back the hands of time. Although it had only been a couple short months I kept thinking, "How long would this unbearable hurt go on. How would we ever be able to live a somewhat normal life without Susan?"

Chapter 21. The Party Continues

I had a very enjoyable thirtieth birthday. I was very glad Stephanie organized it and gathered up all my family and friends. After the party ended, Ashley wanted me to head over to her house for a while since she was unable to stop by the party. I told her I would swing by for a few moments. I got over there shortly after 10 p.m. She was there with her boyfriend, Kevin, and Shannon. I wouldn't exactly fall in love this night, but I soon realized I had met the girl of my dreams. Ashley was in need of an air mattress, so we all piled in my car and headed to the dreaded Wal-Mart. When we arrived back at Ashley's house, we decided we were going to play Twister. Kevin didn't want to play, so Shannon and I played while Ashley spun the wheel. Through all I had dealt with these past two months, it was nice to finally have some fun times. I ended up staying over there until 7 the next morning, which quite worried my dad. I never thought to call. I know now I should have, but again another lapse in judgment. This was definitely a time of my life I wasn't looking to fall in love, I wasn't even looking for anyone to date; however, it wouldn't take long before I would fall head over heels in love. I needed someone in my life desperately. I finally found someone whom I didn't say, "She ain't Alena." Trying to console my mother was becoming overwhelming, and I needed to share my

thoughts with someone other than her. My parents were engulfed with grief and it was weighing on me trying to keep it all together.

The following Sunday, Shannon and I went on our first official date. From then on, we would be connected at the hip. We met at a little Japanese restaurant in Shelby then went to her grandparents house. For the next hour we sat in my car, and I talked about the incident with her. It was at this time, I began to realize I needed her in my life as much or more than I wanted her. Usually, I was off work on Sundays and Wednesdays, so you know who I was spending my time with on these days. We played miniature golf in Black Mountain the following Wednesday and again discussed the incident for over an hour. She told me about how her dad lost his brother in a car wreck when he was thirty. This was destiny…surely she could fix me. On Friday evening, I spent the night with her. Shannon, her brother Nick, and myself all watched "Twilight." This was the first night I ever kissed her and I knew I was falling quickly. It wasn't long after that, I took Shannon to the scene of the wreck. Surely, she could help me figure out and understand what happened that day.

They shot fireworks at the mall on July 3rd this year and Emily asked if I wanted to watch them. I let her know I was going with my family, but she was welcome to join us. She did and talked about how she had broken up with her boyfriend a few days earlier. She's a very nice

girl, but I felt weird hanging out with her tonight when I was beginning to fall for Shannon. The fireworks were beautiful, but I couldn't help thinking about the fireworks I was experiencing with Shannon. The next day would be the 4th of July, Susan's favorite holiday and the first holiday since the incident. At least now I had something else to take up part of my mind and time.

Rhonda made a comment that this was one of the first holidays in a while everyone was there.

Granny replied, "Well not everyone, we are missing two from last year."

Not only had we lost my sister in a tragic accident, my uncle lost his battle to cancer just a few months earlier. It had been quite a year for our family and the year was far from over. While sitting in the gazebo like we did every 4th of July, Andrew asked me to get him a refill. I replied, "Normally we would have someone that would get whatever we wanted." Baffled, he wondered who and immediately got quiet realizing whom I was referring. At least Shannon was texting me throughout the night to keep my mind off the absence of Susan. Wow…I needed Shannon in my life so bad right now!

No one directly spoke about Susan today. We can't just forget she ever existed! We can't simply stop thinking or talking about her! Do they ever think about her anymore? Have they simply forgot she was always the life of the party? I don't know if they think they will offend

us if they talk about her or if they think it will hurt our feelings. It's hard to know if it will or not. I don't think we could be hurt much more than we have been these past couple of months. I try to put myself in their shoes and realize it must be hard to know what to say. However, saying nothing certainly isn't helping us.

It was vacation time…and Susan wouldn't be able to go with us this year. We decided to go to Pigeon Forge for a few days. It was very relaxing, but also very upsetting Susan wasn't with us. I would not be able to tell her about this new girl I had met. I couldn't explain how I had found someone I wanted to marry as much as I did Alena. She would not be able to give me any advice.

Mom and I sat on a swing and watched as a mother duck took care of her six children. I sat out there for hours, lost in my thoughts, and watching the ducks waddle in the river. The next day one of the ducks was missing. This really upsets my momma. I couldn't help but wonder, were they grieving now for their loss like we were for ours?

The next two months I would completely fall in love with 'Mighty Mite.' My parents seemed to be fussing more and more over trivial things, and Shannon would help me more than she could ever comprehend. She became my outlet and my source of escape. She was able to relieve some of the stress and tension I was dealing with. Within the first six weeks of meeting her, I was telling her how much I loved

her, looking at houses together, and planning our wedding. Soon right!? It was…I realize this. However, I was so afraid that something bad would happen to her as well. After all, Susan was killed at such a young age. I had already lost Eric. Alena had already ripped my heart out. Alena was after all, my first true love. I didn't want to have to imagine living my life without Shannon too. Seems like everyone I get close to in my life doesn't last. Every time I left Shannon's house, I truly missed her and couldn't wait to be with her again. I mean, Shannon gave me something else to think about, something wonderful in my life, something I could hold on to. I really thought she was 'the one.' I didn't want to have to think about being without her. She made me feel loved and special.

I had met Shannon's family several times by now and loved speaking with her dad. With him being through a similar situation, I felt he truly understood what I was dealing with and could help me cope with my feelings. Unlike most people who are only able to sympathize with you, I felt he earnestly empathized for me. After all, he was a member of the same club I was. I was able to relate with him and he could relate with me. I began expecting Shannon to understand what I was dealing with also and be able to fill a huge void. I clung to her with every fiber in my body. I desperately needed her in my life.

Unlike my first few encounters with Shannon's family, she would have a very unusual

first few meetings with mine. We had just left the scene of the accident when Dad called, saying we were going to pick out Susan's tombstone. Wow…how would you like to meet your boyfriend's parents under these circumstances? They would be many shoes we would expect Shannon to fill over the next few months…shoes no one would be able to. Not only would she meet my parents in such an eerie way, I wanted her to help pick out the tombstone. After all, I expected Shannon to be part of the family for many years to come. I expected her to be my future wife. The next weekend she spent the night with my family and my parents insisted she sleep in Susan's room. We had not opened her door since the incident, and I told Mom I would sleep on the couch and she could sleep in my bed. They saw no reason for me to sleep on the couch when we had two beds upstairs. My mom even told Shannon if she wanted any of Susan's clothes she was welcome to them.

It was only a few weeks later we went to a family's house that were at the scene of the accident. They tried to provide us with some details of that tragic day but were unable to answer many of the questions we had. Why did Susan have to die so young? Does anyone care my life is completely shattered? Needless to say, Shannon was thrown into a unique situation…a situation that would eventually become overwhelming.

Thankfully, Shannon not only helped time fly by throughout the rest of the summer, she was

able to help me cope to a certain degree and relieve some unbearable stress and tension I was dealing with. Once the summer ended; however, we began facing issues. She was back in school working two jobs. I was working long hours at the store and we had less time to spend with each other. I still wanted and needed to spend all my free time with her, but she was overwhelmed with her workload. I still expected her to be able to fix me. I don't know why I thought anyone could fix me. I don't even know what there was to fix. However, her dad had been through this same thing, surely she would have or could get the answers I needed. As I felt her drifting away, I held on tighter and tighter. I couldn't stand the thought of losing her too. How could I possibly live my life without Shannon as well.

September was coming to a close and I felt like our relationship was too. I had to do something to hang on to Shannon, anything. Her birthday was fast approaching and I wanted to get her something extra special. She had to work late on her birthday, so I decided to surprise her. I drove up to see her with flowers and balloons. For some reason, she didn't seem too excited to see me and that was when I really became worried that our relationship was coming to an end. I tried to do anything to maintain our love…anything not to lose Shannon too.

It was now time for Wesley and Emilee's wedding. This would be a very difficult weekend for my family. They would marry on the day before Susan's birthday. Shannon and I had

planned on going for months and she looked so beautiful all dressed up. The ceremony and reception were beautiful, just like the girl of my dreams. After the reception, we went back to my house and talked about Susan's birthday. I really needed Shannon to be with me tomorrow to help keep my mind off things. She had to be at work early the next morning and informed me she had lots of school work to complete that afternoon. She would not visit me that day or any day in the future. I was devastated Shannon, my girlfriend, wouldn't come visit me on this very difficult day. I contacted Eric's dad, Ricky, this afternoon and hoped I could speak with him. I sadly told him it was Susan's birthday and I was having a very difficult time coping. I knew he would be able to provide me with some words of comfort. We spoke for nearly two hours and he was able to make me feel a little better. He was at least someone who truly knew what I was dealing with and was willing to listen.

Chapter 22. True Love Doesn't Fade

Obviously, fall was in the air. Leaves were falling off the trees, the air was getting cooler, and the butterflies were finding warmer places to dwell. October had come to a close, Halloween had passed, and Thanksgiving was fast approaching. It was November 4th and I had decided to go to the chiropractor. I was tired of my back killing me every day and surely a chiropractor could give me some sort of much needed relief. I would soon realize the enormous emotional strain I had been dealing with these past few months was causing just as much of my back pain as the physical strain. I met with the doctor and received an initial check up and adjustment. I must admit, it did help my back feel some what better for a short while. I went to Shannon's this afternoon to see her once again. She had just gotten her hair cut, and as usual, she was absolutely eye catching. I spent a couple hours with her and left to let her get some school work done.

Now it was time for inventory. This was a day I dread each year. So much preparing, so much work, such an early, long day. The previous two years I had won the loss prevention award at the company meeting for having one of the lowest shrinks and best inventory results in the company. However, this would be the first year the loss prevention manager would assist

with inventory. I arrived at the store around 5:30 in the morning and Don, the loss prevention manager, arrived shortly after. From the moment he walked in, he was complaining about one thing or the other. He insisted the store wasn't properly prepped. He was very aggravated the inventory team was over an hour late. When the inventory team finally arrived, he was frustrated at how few of a staff they brought with them. Although I had little control over many of these issues, it seemed like I couldn't do anything to please him. I found this very annoying, after all, I had always been in charge of my own inventory and had always had better than sufficient results.

Finally, inventory was complete and we had straightened the store back up from the mess the inventory team had left. It was slightly after 1 p.m. and I was planning on visiting Shannon the rest of the afternoon. I got back to my car to head home and check to see if I had any messages on my phone. I had three text messages from Shannon. I assumed they were about what we were doing that afternoon. Unfortunately, I would be gravely mistaken.

> "I've been doing a lot of thinking lately…bout how I haven't been giving you the time and attention you want/deserve…and my schedule next semester is going to be worse cuz I have a Wednesday evening class and on Monday mornings I gotta be at work in Black Mountain at 6 a.m. so Sundays I'll be getting in bed early…so…maybe we

> should take a break…til I'm done with school…I don't want to hurt you…I care a lot about you…you deserve to be happy and right now I can't be what you want right now…I can still be there for you to talk to."

Obviously, this wasn't the message I was expecting and most certainly not the one I needed to hear at this time of my life. For the next few hours I tried contacting Shannon but was unable to reach her. Finally, I got a hold of her desperately seeking some sort of explanation. She simply said, she didn't think I was 'the one' for her, and obviously I didn't understand. How could she say she loved me every day and send me pictures of the wedding dress she wanted if I wasn't 'the one'? Why would she go look at houses with me and talk about getting married? There wasn't anything I wouldn't have done for her, and no one I needed more in my life. I had just about come to grips with losing my sister, and this not only created a new wound, it reopened the wound I thought she was healing. Shannon may have just been a band-aid for a gaping wound, but she had provided much needed comfort and relief.

The next day at work I saw Denise, from church, in the store and desperately wanted to speak to her. I was hoping she would be able to provide me with some sort of comfort. I was unable to muster up any words to say to her or even get the courage to come out of the back

room. I knew if I did, I would break down and I didn't want anyone seeing me get this emotional. I was unable to eat anything for the next few days and didn't feel like doing anything but lay in bed. At this moment in time, I truly felt my world was coming to an end. I really didn't think I could go on living without both Shannon or Susan in my life, but I had to for my mama. I felt like I would have to climb up just to reach the bottom of the barrel.

Having to deal with the death of my sister was an unbearable task. However, losing the one that helped me deal with this was insurmountable. I felt like Shannon simply abandoned me because she couldn't deal with the pain I was going through. If you can't be with someone through the entire grief process, don't be with them through any of it. It seemed everyone in my life I had ever loved were vanishing. When Susan died, I had hundreds of people to console me. Unfortunately, when Shannon ripped my heart out there was no one to pick up the pieces.

The very day after Shannon ripped out my heart and shattered my world, it had come to my attention that Jesse would not face any other charges. How could there not at least be a trial? How could he not at least be held accountable for his actions? How could this not be considered vehicular manslaughter? Accident or not, certainly he was negligent. Surely, this tragedy could have been prevented! Did the police even investigate or was this just another report they

must complete? I felt like no one cared, no one wanted to own up for what happened!

The next week I saw Patty at the bank, and I let her know Shannon had broken up with me. She informed me that my mom had let her know at their church meeting and was very worried. I hugged Patty and began to cry.

How could I have lost two people I loved more than anything in the world in such a short time frame? How would I ever find it in my heart to love again? Why was everyone close to me falling out of my life? How would I possibly survive this? What if something bad happens to Stephanie? My biggest fear now is something tragic will happen to her. There is no way I could live my life without her too. I can't let this consume my mind, but how can't I feel this way? Seems like everyone I truly love disappears from my life!

Chapter 23. Christmas Will Be Different this Year

It was Thanksgiving again. Stephanie and Nelson were visiting his family in Virginia and would not be at Granny's for this holiday. The entire morning and afternoon I wrote Christmas cards to almost everyone in the church. I wanted to let them know just how much their thoughts, prayers, and concerns meant to me over these past few months. I tried to personalize each card to let them know exactly how much I had grown to love them. I not only thought of Floyd's Creek Baptist as the church I attended, it had become a part of my extended family. I grew closer and closer to the church and the members who went there. I would complete nearly half of the Christmas cards this day and gained a new appreciation for the true meaning of Thanksgiving. This not only made me feel better, it also helped pass the time on this first Thanksgiving without Susan.

This evening we went to Granny's house, like we did every major holiday. We had our normal meal and our typical conversation. However, this was not your typical holiday for me. This would be the first holiday I would be the only sibling at our get together. Fortunately, we had lots of good conversation and played several games of UNO to pass the time. We always draw names on Thanksgiving to determine who we need to get a Christmas gift

for. My family debated for a while whether we would include our names or not this year. We finally decided we would since we didn't want to change our entire routine. I was thankful to draw Andrew's name again this year. I knew it would be easy to find something he would like without much effort. I still didn't like going shopping. I always used to go shopping with Susan. Fortunately, I was able to find something at the store I managed that I thought would be perfect for Andrew. We tried to keep everything as close to normal as we could. Of course, as I've mentioned many times, keeping things normal, as they say, wasn't easy.

The next morning was Black Friday. I had to be at the store at 5:30 for the early bird special. I arrived to work and was unable to get the cash register working. Great…already off to a bad start! Shortly after opening, Kyra stopped in to purchase some items for Christmas. I begged her to go to Radio Shack to find a new keyboard. She came back within an hour with a new one but it wasn't compatible with our register system. Finally, after a few more minutes of working on the keyboard, I was able to get the register up and running. What a way to start off this day!

For lunch, my parents picked me up, and we went out to eat. Since the incident, I tried to eat lunch with my family as much as possible, especially Stephanie. At least twice a week I made a point to eat lunch with Stephanie, which I really enjoyed. As we were driving downtown, I

saw someone I swear was Shannon. I yelled for Dad to turn the car around. I had to see if this was her with another guy in my hometown. Thank goodness it wasn't. Obviously, I was still completely hung up on her.

The next few weeks were very busy at the store...everyone completing their last minute Christmas shopping. I was glad for this, kept my mind off the troubles going on in my life. I finally finished my Christmas cards to everyone at church, as well as many of our customers at the store and decided to write Shannon a long letter. I hadn't spoken to her or had any contact with her since we had broken up. I wasn't exactly trying to get her back, but I did want to let her know what I was still feeling. I honestly believe if you are ever truly in love with someone you can't simply fall out of love. I was also hoping for some sort of reply. Unfortunately, I never heard from her or what was going on in her life. Does she not know, she was still a major thought on my mind? Does she not realize how much I loved her, how much I still loved her, how much I'll always love her? Did she ever love me at all or was it all just a facade? Had she simply fallen out of my life like everyone else I had ever truly cared for? Did she ever think about me anymore, like I always thought about her?

It was Christmas Eve now, and the store was slam full of people. I was glad this day flew by. Now it was time to count down the register and head to my Granny's house for our

Christmas celebration. Emilee and Wesley weren't going to be there this year; they went to visit her family in Michigan. This holiday was especially hard without Susan. Me and her would always stay up late talking about life and what we hoped to get for Christmas. This year I wasn't able to have that talk. I was unable to share with her what had been going on in my life. I couldn't tell her about Shannon and how she had ripped my heart out like Alena had. Was it possible that somehow she knew despite the fact she was no longer with us? Was it possible that she looks down upon me and weeps when I weep? Do you think it's possible that just like a caterpillar transforming into a beautiful butterfly she has become a Heavenly angel? I mean, every single day I wear the angel pin her friend gave me in the hospital to give to Susan when she got better. However, Susan didn't get better! I couldn't give this gift to her, so I must wear it as a constant reminder. Could Susan be my guardian angel? Could she watch over me when I'm hurting, sad, or need someone to talk to?

I fall asleep this evening with a heavy weight on my heart. I wake up the next morning, but unlike most Christmas mornings I had no presents under the tree. We decided not to even put our stockings out this year. It was a very unusual Christmas morning…it had been a very unusual year. Unlike most years, Stephanie and Nelson came over for lunch. Our hearts were still very heavy and everyone else seemed to have moved on with their lives like nothing had

changed. Did people not realize we were still hurting…we were still in desperate need of prayers? Did they not realize we not only lost someone we cared deeply for, we had lost part ourselves, part of our heart, mind, and sanity? Could anyone hear our cries and feel our hurt when we could barely even speak or explain how much anguish we were still feeling? How could anyone possibly realize how much grief we were still dealing with?

Holidays are obviously difficult for us, but at least this is a time we aren't alone. At least we have family surrounding us during these occasions. Although no one speaks of Susan on these days, or any days for that matter, she is thought about quite often. At least for myself, I think about her all the time! Some people may say the holidays are the worse, but for me, it's not the holidays that are as difficult as the days in between. These are the days where I must be alone to drown in my own thoughts. The times I realize I no longer have Susan or Shannon in my life. These are the times I desperately need someone to talk with. Who can console me now; where can I find peace in this time of despair?

Chapter 24. A New Year But Not A New Beginning

It was New Years Eve…a time for most people to make their New Years resolutions and a chance to have a new beginning. It was a particularly slow day at work. However, just before closing two young girls entered the store and attempted to steal a pair of sandals. It took the police nearly thirty minutes to arrive at the store. After all, it was New Years Eve and all the crazies were out and about. When the police finally did arrive to the store, the girls tried denying any involvement in this crime. I let the officers know what they had taken and where they had placed it. They searched the purses of the young girls and found the pair of sandals they had not paid for. They also found some cigarettes and alcohol they had stolen from Wal-Mart. Since they were under eighteen, it took the police nearly an hour to complete the police report and place this charge on their permanent records.

Finally, nearly an hour after close, I was able to leave the store. Winters was having several people over to watch some football and ring in the New Year. I enjoyed this time of fellowship. It was nice to get away from reality…if it was only for a night. I headed home shortly before lunch time the next morning. Stephanie and Nelson came over for the traditional New Years meal of black-eyed peas,

collard greens, and cornbread. This was not particularly one of my favorite meals, but it was tradition and we couldn't break tradition.

The next several weeks went by like every other day the past nine months, very slowly. I left work early one particularly slow day and headed for the house. Unfortunately, for some reason or other, I was in an extreme hurry to arrive home and get pulled over by the highway patrol. Like many other days over the past few months, my mind was simply drifting back to that tragic day in April. Needless to say, I was flying home on this particular afternoon. The police clocked me at 66 in a 35 and threatened to take my license. For the next couple of months, I was consulting with lawyers, officers, and friends about my options. After much discussion, I chose a lawyer I thought gave me the best hope of keeping my license and reducing my consequences. Not only did I have to hire the services of a lawyer, I had to attend an eight hour driving course on a Saturday to keep my license. This process went on for over three months before I finally had my day in court and was able to get the ticket reduced to 49 in a 35, which kept it from being a reckless driving charge. Unfortunately, this did still put two points on my license and raised the rates on my insurance.

It was the end of January now and my dad was turning sixty. We hadn't really discussed his birthday too much. With everything else that had gone on the past nine months, his birthday, like

so many other things, had just slipped up on us. A few days before his big day, I decided to throw him a surprise party. I contacted all the family and several of his friends. We decided to have his party at Big Dave's, and it came up a huge snow storm. The entire day I was contacting everyone to let them know we would move the party up an hour in order to get back home before the roads got too bad. I placed a few balloons on Susan's jeep, the vehicle my dad was now driving to work, and prepared for the festivities. Due to the inclement weather, it wasn't until the last minute I knew if we were going to be able to keep the party on as scheduled. Fortunately, everyone was able to attend the celebration and boy was my dad surprised. It took lots of convincing from Mom and myself to get Dad out of the house. He did not want to get out in such a bad snow storm. I excitedly told him we had to take him out for his sixtieth birthday. Thankfully, we were finally able to convince him and we all had a great time.

January had come to an end, and I decided to sign up for E-harmony. I was still not completely over Shannon but thought it would do me some good to meet a quality girl. The very first day I signed up, I was introduced to Beth Ann. We went through the entire E-harmony process within a week and began chatting on Facebook. During this entire week, Mom kept referring to her as 'Grin.' I always had a smile on my face when chatting with her. We decided to meet at the Cracker Barrel in Spartanburg on

February 13th. Yea, I know what you are thinking, why would you go on your first date the day before Valentines? Nevertheless, we had a good meal and decided to go to Westgate Mall for a little while. I talked about the incident quite a bit and I also mentioned Shannon. I wanted to let her know I was not 100 percent over her but was ready to move on. At least, I thought I was ready to move on.

I drove down to Greenville to see Beth Ann a few weeks later. There were so many crosses on the side of the road. So many families must be feeling the way I was feeling. Hard to imagine how many people must be in my club. People I had never seen or would never know, yet had a heartfelt compassion for. One cross had a picture of a young girl and read, "We Love You Dena." It went on to say she had died in '94. I didn't know her, but I hurt for her family the way they would mine. It had been sixteen years since they lost their loved one, but I knew they still thought about her daily. I knew they still grieve for Dena like I still grieve for my best friend that died over seventeen years ago now. I passed by these crosses weekly and every time I saw one on the side of the road, I couldn't help but think about Susan. Of course, I think about her all the time, but these crosses constantly reminded me of how she was way too young to be taken so tragically. Before the incident, I never really paid much attention to crosses on the side of the road. Now, I truly ache for the families who have lost a loved one in such a

tragic way.

Suffering goes on all over the world, and we are only vaguely aware of it. However, when tragedy strikes us it sharpens our senses and we begin to notice suffering in the lives of others more intently than we ever had in the past. We not only sympathize with those hurting, we become much more empathetic for those in pain and truly care about their well-being.

Chapter 25. Freak Accident

Basketball season had rolled back around and this was the first year we placed a team in the Forest City league. I had been having a pretty good season so far. My last two games I scored twenty-four and twenty-six. I was averaging eighteen points a game and shooting fairly well. However, everything would change on February 8th. We were playing one of the top teams in the league. Our team was struggling, and I was trying to get something started. I went for a loose ball and took an elbow to the jaw. The next few minutes became very hazy. I lay on the court for several minutes and could not walk off on my own power. Two of my teammates carried me to the bench and one of the refs tried to keep me alert. I was feeling very woozy and wanted to fall asleep. The ref assured me I didn't need to doze off. He assessed my injuries and continued speaking with me. For some reason, I was unable to move my arms or legs. They were very tingly. I could feel my limbs, but had no movement at all. The EMS arrived within twenty minutes and Chris St. Claire was the first responder once again. He was, as you recall, the first responder in Susan's accident. Just a few months earlier I had hired his girlfriend, Chelsea, to work with me. At the time, I had no idea they were dating. We had to stop running into each other this way, I thought to myself. At first, he didn't remember me. Did he not remember that

tragic day last April? They performed several generic tests on me and did everything in their power to get me to move my arms and legs. Nothing! This was obviously very scary for myself and my parents, who were in the crowd watching me play this evening. Eventually, they carried me off on a stretcher. By the time I arrived to the ambulance, I was regaining some movement in my arms but still had no movement at all in my legs. The doctors were unable to explain why I couldn't move my legs or why my arms were still very tingly like I had hit my funny bone. I knew I wasn't paralyzed since I did have feeling in all my body parts. However, why could I not move my legs? How long would it be before I could walk again?

Once I arrived at the hospital, the doctors took me for an MRI and all results came back normal. Of course, it was by no means normal not to be able to fully move. The doctors diagnosed me with a concussion, but still had no explanation for the lack of movement in my extremities. They wanted to send me to Asheville for further tests. I absolutely did not want to go back up to that hospital. I did not regain movement in my legs for over three hours after the accident. Fortunately, the doctors discharged me and told me to rest for a few days. I was unable to go to work the next day and really couldn't do much more than lay on the couch. That Wednesday, I went to the chiropractor and they took X-rays of my neck and back to reassess my injuries. The X-rays

showed I had chipped a bone in one of the vertebrae in my neck. The doctors informed me that it should never be a problem unless I take another blow to the head. What would happen if I did take another shot to the head? Was this a chance I was willing to take? I couldn't just sit on the sidelines from now on. I was way too active and enjoy sports too much to simply be a spectator. The next few games, however, I could be no more than a spectator for my team. Fortunately, we were in the weakest section of our schedule and were able to prevail in all these games. During these weeks, I had extreme dizzy spells and several headaches. I could do little more than stand up without feeling like I was going to fall down. Climbing ladders was a very tricky task, but one I had no choice but to perform while at work. I continued going to the chiropractor weekly and voicing my concerns about these dizzy spells. My chiropractor was very concerned as well, but like the doctors had no explanations or suggestions. No one seemed to understand what was going on with my body.

I began playing a few minutes a game over the next few weeks, but was still having dizzy spells and unable to play long periods of time. I was unable to play at my typical level for the rest of the season. After three months, the dizzy spells and headaches had virtually disappeared and it seemed my body was finally getting back to some sort of normality.

Chapter 26. Has It Been A Year Already?

It was April again, and we all knew how difficult of a month this would be. April Fools Day, the day everyone makes a joke out of something. However, our past year had been anything but a joke. It had been surreal for certain, even dream like, but this is the kind of dream you always hope to wake up from. The past year had been a blur, so many ordeals and obstacles to overcome. Not only had I lost my sister, whom I cared about more than anything, I had lost the girl of my dreams. If that wasn't bad enough, I was still having to fight that speeding ticket I received several months back, and I was trying to recover from the chipped bone in my neck. Surely, things are bound to look up for me soon.

Easter Sunday was supposed to be a time of joy, a time of hope. For me though, it was a constant reminder this was the last time my sister would ever be home…the last holiday she was the life of our family gatherings. It's always difficult saying goodbye. People kept telling me the first year would be the hardest. Well it was fast approaching a year now on this tragic event and I was still not ready to say goodbye. I was still not ready to accept I would never be able to talk to Susan again, never be able to laugh with her, or see that upside down smile.

It was April 6th today, a day I always

dread coming around. However, like every other day, this day must come, but it also must pass. This was the first time this wasn't the anniversary of the worse day of my life, now it was not even the anniversary of the worse day of the month. Now though, I not only thought about my best friend Eric, I also remembered my sister. How can one person possibly carry this much weight on their heart? I didn't have Shannon to talk to any more, and I was fearful to get too attached to Beth Ann. After all, it was too much for Shannon to bear…it would probably be too much for Beth Ann to deal with as well. It was too much for anyone to understand. I kept placing unrealistic expectations on people, expecting them to be able to fully understand what I was dealing with. I couldn't even grasp everything I had dealt with this past year but expected others to. How could they possibly comprehend what was going on in my mind? However, I still wanted them to! I still wanted them to say how everything was going to be alright. I needed to know they truly cared and were earnestly concerned for me and my well-being. I knew it wasn't fair for me to think my problems were bigger or more important than theirs, but it was so difficult for me to take on anyone else's stress or issues right now.

April 17th fell on a Saturday this year. This was the last time I ever truly saw Susan. Yea…we saw her in the hospital for several days after, but was she even really at the hospital? Was that really her clinging to life? Was she not

already in Heaven singing with the angels? I recollected the memories of this day last year. I was so glad we had a wonderful time with no arguments. This was a day we would never forget! This was a great day I could always remember…remember how Susan flagged us down and directed us into a parking space with her unique smile. A time I could remember her talking about traveling around the world.

I couldn't believe it had been an entire year since the incident. So many events had happened over the past year, so many of which were little more than a blur to me now. Very many of which I wished I could change. How could Shane be preaching his last sermon on this day? How could he be going to a new church? Did he not realize I still needed him, our family still needed him? Was it running through his mind right now, that this time last year he wasn't preparing for a sermon but a funeral? Was he thinking about Susan today like me and my family were?

The next day at work I was very distraught. I called Melony and discouragingly told her I didn't know if I could continue as the store manager. I just couldn't focus any more. I was not the manager I once was. How long would I be hurting? How much more could I withstand? I went on to say that this Thursday would be the one year anniversary of Susan's death. I knew how tough this week would be, but could never imagine all the grief I would be dealing with or how much hurt I would still be

feeling.

The dreaded Thursday morning was finally here. With any luck, since it was shipment day, it would pass fairly quickly. I certainly hoped so. I couldn't deal with much more grief. Shortly after opening both Melony and Don arrived. I found it strange they both showed up on shipment day but didn't think much about it. After all, I had much more important things on my mind this day. Melony informed me it was time for my yearly evaluation. How could she possibly do this today? Last year she had to conduct this critique just after Susan passed away and now she chose the one year anniversary to go over it with me. We went back to my makeshift office and went over the yearly evaluation. She informed me I was an above average manager and gave me a raise. Above average! Wow…how could I possibly still be an above average manager with everything I had went through and all the mistakes I had certainly made this past year?

Immediately after Melony completed the evaluation, Don came in needing to speak with me for a few moments. I had no clue what this was in regards to. He acquired about several unusual layaway transactions. I explained to him that on three separate occasions the register was short. It was short $10 twice and $30 once. I further explained I transferred money from outstanding layaway payments into the register to balance out the cash drawer. He questioned why I would do that? I stated these payments were

from 2007 or older and this money was simply in an idle account. In order for the drawer not to be short, I simply placed money from this idle account into an active account. After speaking with several people at the home office, Don informed me this was not the correct way of handling this situation. I adamantly stated I had never been shown this was incorrect and questioned where in policy it stated this was wrong. He asked if I thought I should have to return the money.

I forcefully exclaimed, "Absolutely not! I didn't take any money or give out any money. I was simply balancing out the register!"

It was at this time he informed me, it was time to part ways. He didn't even say he was firing me or letting me go, he said 'part ways.'

"I can't believe you are doing this today of all days. Do you not have a heart? Do you not care about your employees or have any compassion at all? After all I've done for this company. All the hard work and sacrifice."

It was then I realized this company truly cared more about the bottom line than their hard working employees. I also realized you can do everything in your power to make a company more successful, but if you make one minor mistake or have one lapse in judgment that is what corporate America focuses on. They don't care about all the money you have helped earn for their company or all the sacrifices you have made. How ironic is it that I get a raise on the same day I get fired or as they say, 'parted

ways?'

As I was leaving the store, I shook Scott, Kyra, and Justin's hands and sincerely told them it had been a pleasure working with them these past few years. It truly had. I was always blessed with an outstanding group of people to work with. I tried to hold in my emotions until I got to the car. I couldn't let anyone see me cry. I had put in so much work for this company. I not only took this as a job…I thought of it as my life. Granted, over the past twelve months, I had reevaluated many aspects of my life and attempted to put my priorities in order. However, I still cared deeply for the success of this store, the store that I had vastly improved. As I got to my car, I begged to God why my life was falling to pieces? Why have I had so much to deal with over the past year? Was I Job, from the Bible? Was He testing me? How much could one man lose before he loses himself?

I didn't know whom to call or what to do. Shannon was always able to console me through the ordeal with Susan and I thought maybe she could help me now. I hadn't spoken to her for months and tried not to show emotion when I called her up. Unfortunately, with all I was dealing with, I had no choice but to let my emotions out. I simply told her I felt like my world was crashing down around me. She questioned whether I had seen a counselor, and I confessed that was what she was supposed to be. After all, wasn't she supposed to be able to fix me? Wasn't she the one I was supposed to

marry? However, it was obvious she didn't care about me anymore, maybe she never did. If she had cared, would she have reopened the hole she never could fill?

I went over to Nelson's this afternoon. I had to get away from my thoughts. We talked for a while about what I wanted in life. I wanted what everyone wants, to be truly happy. Was that too much to ask…was that too much to pray for? Even the butterflies I saw on this spring afternoon seemed to be happy. They were so peaceful flying from one plant to the next. There were two of them playing together. Oh, what joy to be a simple butterfly! No worries, no concerns, just able to enjoy the beautiful world that surrounds us. We take this world for granted so often. Consumed with our everyday problems and concerns. Overwhelmed with grief, stress, and worry. Caught up in the mundane day to day activities. Just the day before, I had placed an offer on a house. Fortunately, I was able to back out on this deal. I guess once again, buying a house would have to wait. As bad as this day was, it still wasn't the worse April 22nd I'd ever faced.

The next day I stayed in bed virtually all day. I had no energy to do much of anything. I had worked so hard and so long for so many years now. I just wanted to lay in bed, catch up on some much needed rest, and reevaluate the thoughts running through my mind.

I filed my unemployment for the first time this Sunday. I was informed it may take a

couple of weeks before receiving any benefits. Very strange feeling filing unemployment. I had always been one to do my best at whatever I attempted. I felt almost like a failure admitting I lost my job. I felt like I couldn't even fully function without Susan around.

I didn't begin looking for jobs right away. I tried to reevaluate what I really wanted in life and what type of job best suited me. The entire next week after losing my job, I cleaned out as much as possible in the house. I not only cleaned my room, I cleaned out the attic, basement, and closets. I figured if I was not working, I might as well stay productive. It surprisingly only took a week to get most of the clutter out of the house. It's surprising how much one can accomplish when one sets their mind to something. I took two truckloads of trash to the dump. It's amazing at how much stuff overtakes your house in twenty-two years.

I called human resources asking for a copy of the policy I supposedly broke. They would not provide me with one or even explain to me what I was being let go for. I inquired about retrieving my personal belongings and they informed me Melony must be present. How could they possibly be treating me like a criminal after all the hard work I had done for this company? I hope they struggle without me. I want them to realize how valuable I was to this store and this company. One week after I lost my job, I went back to the store to pick up my personal belongings. Melony had it all boxed up

and had removed everything out of my briefcase. I never expected to be at the same job my entire life, but I surely didn't think this was how I would be forced to leave. Not only did they let me go on the worse day imaginable, but they were doing everything in their power to make this as difficult as possible. I also spoke with human resources about my three weeks paid vacation and awards from the company meeting I was to attend. They informed me both of these would be forfeited and again gave me no explanation or policy stating the reason behind this decision.

It was time to observe Memorial Day now. As we were leaving church, Dad began to pull around to the cemetery. I questioned what he was doing and he insisted he wanted to see the flowers on Susan's grave. I hadn't been to the grave since the funeral, and I desperately didn't want to today. I glance out the window on occasion as I go to my Sunday School class, but I wouldn't dare go to her grave. I couldn't bring myself to go to the place where I saw them put her body in the ground.

During the summer, I began doing research on head trauma victims. I wanted to know the ins and outs of brain injuries. I felt like if I knew exactly what happened to my sister, I would find some comfort and perhaps be able to help someone in the future. Although she was no longer with us, I still felt I could find something the doctors had missed. I have no doubt they did everything in their power to help save her;

however, it wasn't their sister. There were several experimental procedures and some ideas I had that I thought could have saved her life. However, even if her life could have been saved it's uncertain of the quality of life she could have lived. One thing was quite certain, she would have never been the same Susan we all loved.

Several weeks had passed now and I still hadn't received any money from unemployment. My last check had just went into my account, and now I had no income coming in. I had applied to nearly fifty jobs already. Finally, I began getting a few interviews. Things were beginning to look up. I was starting to think I would get a job fairly soon and wouldn't have to worry about unemployment or losing my job. My first interview was with Wachovia and immediately I knew being let go from my previous job was going to present challenges. They couldn't get over the fact I was let go for a 'policy violation.' Despite the fact I was a very hard working manager for over eight years with a college degree, they couldn't see past one blemish on my record…a blemish I still felt was unjustified or fair. It didn't take long before I had several other interviews. The week after my interview with Wachovia, both Dick's Sporting Goods and Family Christian Bookstore called about a management opening. I thought to myself, "This is right up my alley. Surely, I would be perfect for either one of these two positions." Unfortunately, again I was unable to get these jobs. At least I was receiving interviews, I

thought to myself. After all, it was only the first week of May and I'd already had three interviews.

In order to have a little income trickling in, I began working with my best friend, Winters, at Good Shepherd Security Services. I also got a job with Wyzant tutoring a rising ninth grader in algebra. I didn't mind doing this. I had always been very good at math, but it had been over fifteen years since I'd had algebra. The first couple of sessions were not very difficult, but as the material got harder, I had to study more and more to keep up and be able to effectively tutor her. Originally, I was scheduled to tutor her every Thursday in Gaffney, nearly a forty-five minute drive for myself. I didn't mind the drive or the studying that bad, but her mother wouldn't confirm our appointments until after 10 p.m. the night before our session. Eventually, it became more of a burden and hardship than anything else.

Throughout the rest of the summer, I began selling items on the internet we never used anymore. This became a very profitable and enjoyable hobby for myself. Not only was I having fun, I was making a little money as well. By doing this, I was also able to keep myself busy and my mind off all my other worries. However, I was still actively looking for a full-time job and having little success. I was hoping to find a Monday-Friday job in Forest City, but I was applying in Spartanburg and Greenville as well. Obviously, in the horrible economy we

were living in, it was hard to find any job anywhere, much less one that met my criteria and standards.

One good thing that came from not having a job was the opportunity to go on several vacations. Typically, I had always had a difficult time taking a vacation, due to my job. However, this summer I wasn't working and was able to take three separate trips. I was very fortunate to be able to do this and had a very good summer. I was able to go to the beach with Winters and his family for my birthday. It was during this vacation, over seven months since Shannon and I had broken up, that I finally got over her and no longer wanted her back. She didn't even send me a generic birthday card or text, and I didn't want to be with anyone that didn't want to be with me. Obviously, one never completely gets over someone they were in love with, but at least I was now ready to truly move on. Beth Ann was also able to spend a couple of days with me on this trip and a few weeks later I went on a vacation with her family.

At the end of the summer, my family was planning on taking a tour, which I was unsure I would enjoy. Not knowing when my unemployment hearing would be, I was also unaware if I would be able to go on this trip. Thankfully, the week before the tour, I learned my hearing would be on August 4th, two days before leaving on the trip. This was a very enjoyable and relaxing trip. I was able to see lots of places I had never been to before and may

never get to visit again. Shortly after getting back from our vacation, Stephanie let the family know she was going to have a baby and I was going to be an uncle. The joy that came across my family's faces when receiving this news was much needed after the despair that had faced us for so long. I cannot wait to hold this little baby in my arms and of course give her back once I hear a crying voice or smell a dirty diaper.

Chapter 27. I Don't Hear The Wedding Bells

On August 4th, my unemployment case was continued to allow my lawyer time to subpoena some vital documents. My new hearing date had now been moved to September 13th. Less than one week before this hearing, I decided to break it off with Beth Ann. I cared deeply about her but didn't feel she was the one I was to marry. Shannon and I were planning on marrying on September 25th this year and it was a very difficult time for me. I just simply didn't hear the wedding bells. I have had my heart broken a couple times now and didn't want to do that to anyone else, much less someone I had true feelings for. I simply could not bring myself to fall in love with anyone else at this time of my life. I could not risk having my heart broken again. Shannon had hurt me so bad that I distanced myself from Beth Ann. I prayed that God would change my heart towards Beth Ann. I wanted desperately to fall in love. It was just too soon…I'd just had too much hurt these past eighteen months. I didn't need any more stress in my life. Didn't people realize breaking up with her hurt me as well? I empathized with her so much. I know how much she cared about me and how many questions she had running through her mind. I wanted to give her some comfort. I wanted to give her some answers. However, I didn't even have all the answers, so how could I

possibly provide her with any? How could I comfort her when I was still hurting as well? How could I console her when I was the one that hurt her…the one that broke her heart?

The next week my dad and myself drove to Marion for my unemployment hearing. This was the first time I had made this all to familiar drive since Shannon had broken my heart nearly a year earlier. We arrived shortly before the time of my hearing and waited in the lobby. I was very nervous anticipating how this hearing would turn out. Eventually, the hearing officer came out and informed me he had spoken with my lawyer. They decided it would be in my best interest to continue my case, once again due to the fact that the subpoenaed items I requested failed to get subpoenaed on time. Obviously, this annoyed me. I didn't know if the lawyer had dropped the ball or the hearing officer. However, I knew the ball had been dropped and once again I would have to wait for my unemployment fate to be determined.

Finally, it was nearing the end of September and I received a call from 5th/3rd bank saying they were offering me the position. I'd had two interviews for this job and was excited to begin my new career. The customer services manager indicated human resources would be in contact with me soon and get me started in the near future. The following Tuesday the human resource manager did contact me to see if I was still interested in the position. I hadn't worked in over five months and was certainly eager to get

back in the workforce to earn some money. I was beginning to feel like a bum not working. I'd worked since I graduated high school and hated not being able to find a job. The human resource manager indicated I would need to complete an online application for their records, take a drug test, and have a background check. This wasn't an issue for me and I was enthusiastically looking forward to begin my new career. However, she was interested in why I had left my previous job. I indicated I had been seeking other employment for a while, but there was an issue with the register causing them to let me go for an unwritten policy violation. She still wanted me to contact her once I had completed the online application and she would go over the position further with me. It took around an hour to complete, but as soon as I finished, I submitted it, printed off a copy for my records, and contacted human resources. She did not answer so I left a message for her to contact me at her convenience. I hadn't heard from her by the next afternoon and decided to call once again to ensure she had received my application. Again I was unable to reach her and began to worry whether they were going to back out on their original offer. Finally the Saturday I was originally planning on marrying Shannon, the bank called me back. They informed me, due to the nature of my dismissal from my last job, they were reconsidering their original hiring decision. Not wanting to be the bearer of bad news, the customer service manager let me know human

resources would contact me soon to reevaluate the decision. Once again, this couldn't come at a more inopportune time.

The following Monday the human resource manager informed me there was a mistake and I had not received the job. On the same day I was told I no longer had the position at 5th/3rd bank, the supervisor with Farmers Furniture contacted me about a management position. She wanted to know if I would be able to come in for an interview on Friday. I was ecstatic! Not only was this a management position in Forest City, but they closed by 6 every evening. This couldn't be more perfect timing. My hearing was two days prior to my interview and I assumed I would hear the results from it just before learning whether I had this job or not. Unfortunately, the day prior to my interview, the supervisor contacted myself saying she had a death in the family and would need to reschedule our interview for the following week. I totally understood. I knew how difficult it could be to lose a loved one.

After the following week passed and I hadn't heard back from Farmer's Furniture, I decided to contact her to see when a good time would be to reschedule our interview. She didn't answer so I left her a voicemail explaining I was still interested in the position and would like to speak with her further about my career opportunities with this company. Several more days passed and she had yet to return my call. Again, I began thinking something had happened

to change their minds. Finally, two weeks after my original interview was scheduled I get back in touch with the supervisor at Farmer's Furniture. She explained once again she had a death in the family. Always seems like death comes in pairs. She went on to say they were having a company meeting in Georgia and would contact me towards the end of the week to reschedule. Not only did it appear I was going to be having an interview with a local company, but Food Lion called letting me know there was an assistant manager opening in Spartanburg. Around two months prior, I had an interview with Food Lion of Woodruff, but they decided to go with a different candidate. This position was within the same district and the hiring manager explained I was highly recommended for this opening. I also received a call a couple weeks back from my former eighth grade math teacher. She expressed her concerns about how my former employer had treated me. Since she was also a regular customer, she knew how hard I had worked for this company. It was brought to her attention that I was having a difficult time locating another job and she was wanting to help. I was very grateful for any help I could receive. She informed me her brother was a CEO of a major company in Spartanburg and had many connections within the local area. Mrs. Petty then told me to send him a resume, cover letter, and several letters of reference and he would assist me in getting some interviews. I thanked her very much and began thinking things were starting to look up for me

once again.

After five months of not having a job and two continuations on my unemployment, the day had finally come for my case to be heard. I received the information my lawyer had subpoenaed less than four hours before the hearing. I frantically went through the mounds of information to improve my chances. I found several key pieces of information I felt would be beneficial and contacted my lawyer. We reviewed the material over the phone for an hour until it was time to speak with the hearing officer. My lawyer was representing myself over the phone and both Melony and Don were witnesses for my former employer. At the beginning of the hearing, it was brought to our attention that some of the information we requested was not presented to myself or my lawyer. After some debate, we chose to go ahead with the hearing. After all, it had been over five months since I lost my job and I was desperately wanting to hear the outcome of my unemployment case. I also figured the burden of proof was on my former employer to show I was aware I was breaking some sort of policy. The hearing lasted nearly three hours and I felt my case was very strong. The hearing officer informed me he would review all the information and deliver his verdict within a few days.

It was nearing the end of October now. I didn't receive the position at Food Lion, which did not upset me too much. After all, the hours and drive would be long and I would be working

virtually every weekend. Nearly a month had passed since my hearing and I still had not received any word on how it went. I felt like it went very well, but the longer it went with no word, the more worried I became about the outcome. The hearing officer did explain both sides could appeal the decision; however, I really wanted this to be behind me so I could go on with my life.

The last day of October I finally received a call from the unemployment office and was informed I would be receiving all but four weeks of my benefits. The hearing officer had determined my termination was not completely justified. Hopefully, this news would also help in getting a job in the near future. The very next day the manager of Farmers Furniture contacted me letting me know they were offering me the position. After much debate, I chose not to take this offer. Even though it was a good opportunity, it was still retail with long hours. Although I do not currently have a job to keep myself occupied, I have stayed very busy these past few months. I have had the time to do a wide array of things which has been very rewarding.

Chapter 28. Remembering The Good Times

It has been eighteen months now since that tragic day in April. Everyone always says the first year is the hardest. In some ways that was true and in other ways it was far from the truth. Once you get past the first year things will become easier they say. Easier for what…easier for whom? My parents are still having an extremely difficult time coping with this event and I'm finding it harder and harder to know how to help. Every day that passes I still think about my sister, Susan. I'm sure there won't be a day that goes by I don't think about her. However, with every day that passes I gain a deeper appreciation for life. I've learned not to take life for granted, live every day like it may be your last, make friends and memories, and spend as much time as possible with those you love. If there is something you've always wanted to do and always made excuses not to, stop making excuses and start making memories. Don't work on your bucket list when you're 80, 70, 60, or even 50, work on it every day of your life. That way when you become 50, 60, 70, or 80 you'll look back thankful you spent every day to the fullest.

We may never know why one child receives a new bicycle for Christmas while another is diagnosed with cancer. It may be impossible to ever understand how a drunk can

kill someone in a head on collision, yet escape without a scratch. There is obviously no way we can comprehend why one man lives to 100, while a child dies at birth. It's quiet unfair that a parent outlives their child. There are so many questions in this world we will never have the answers to. However, one thing is certain, God sent His only son to take on human life to share our pain and our sorrow. God understands the deep grief of losing a child. He watched as His son died on a cross for our sins. No one ever escapes heartache except for brief periods, yet we stupidly think bad times in life are abnormal and undeserved.

God's will for the world is not evil, but good. It isn't ugliness, but beauty. It certainly isn't tragic accidents for the ones we love, but long productive lives lived in His service and His glory. What God wants for our lives is good, but what we so often choose is not always good. The whole scheme of life has been designed around freedom of choice, the greatest gift of love ever given to a created being. The problem comes because most choices we make involve people other than ourselves.

Our lives are very similar to that of a butterfly. We are born into this world as a helpless baby that needs nurturing from those who love us. Just like a caterpillar, we wander from journey to journey facing many trials and heartaches throughout our days. The life of a caterpillar does not end however at the first glimpse of hopelessness. Despite many devastating trials that we will face, like a

caterpillar, we eventually are able to overcome these obstacles and blossom into a beautiful butterfly. At times, we may think this life is unfair and too difficult, but if the caterpillar had simply given up on life, we would never enjoy the wonders of the butterfly. As beautiful as God's creatures are, we will always be more than a butterfly!

www.ingramcontent.com/pod-product-compliance
Ingram Content Group UK Ltd.
Pitfield, Milton Keynes, MK11 3LW, UK
UKHW020129250726
13967UKWH00002B/547

9 780557 853663